A DEATH DECO
Robert Kennicott
and the
Alaska Telegraph

A Forensic Investigation

Sandra Spatz Schlachtmeyer

ISBN 0976374730

Published and printed in the United States by
Voyage Publishing Inc.
201 North Fairfax Street, Suite 32
Alexandria, Virginia 22314

Designed by Craig Keith

Cover Illustration:
"Loading a Sledge in Alaska" by Frederick Whymper,
Travel and Adventure in the Territory of Alaska, 1868

Back Cover:
Robert Kennicott, 1862
Dr. Douglas Owsley with Kennicott's casket, 2001
Smithsonian Institution, Chip Clark photogtrapher

Contents

Introduction

Robert Kennicott, naturalist and explorer, could also be called the scientist behind the purchase of Alaska: He brought the hope of economic gain to the essentially political decision to acquire Russian America. His two heroic expeditions into the Yukon, from the eastern mountains in 1859 and from the western coast in 1865, brought back reliable information about the numbers and types of fur-bearing animals, the acreage of harvestable forest, and the viability of harbors for commercial shipping.

Kennicott's name appears in most books about the exploration of Alaska because his highly readable reports of his experiences provided some of the first accounts of the area. Kennicott's name is also recognized, although slightly misspelled, in the fabled Kennecott Copper mines. The mother lode was discovered at the foot of Alaska's Kennicott glacier which was named, along with multitudes of other scientific discoveries, by fellow scientists to honor Robert's accomplishments.

Kennicott was uniquely suited to Western Union's plans to span two continents with telegraph wire. Both the corporation and the man valued large-scale operations. Kennicott's often-exuberant personality not only gave him grand visions of what he could accomplish, but also allowed him to convince others of his goals. His infectious enthusiasm for the tasks he undertook swept away any concerns about their difficulty. That can-do attitude pervaded the United States in those years of exploration and expansion; both Western Union and Kennicott embodied the indomitable spirit of the age. That's why the inquiry into Kennicott's death quickly turned into the story of one small group of men in a sprawling corporate undertaking, a venture overlooked in American history largely because it failed. The secondary results of the venture, however, such as increased appreciation of the territory and better mapping of the area, immeasurably helped later entrepreneurs.

Unfortunately, because Kennicott died so young without a long string of honors and without acolytes to enshrine him, his name has slipped from memory. Yet, the Chicago Academy of Sciences he revitalized lives on, with the support and contributions of many others. The specimens of nature he collected and preserved a century ago are still used at the Smithsonian Institution, as comparisons to current specimens. Now, in these pages, and in their own voices through first-person documents, he and his men can take their place among the many whose efforts, bit by incremental bit, built the United States.

The historical story of Kennicott, the Scientific Corps, and Western Union as they all attempted to construct a telegraph line through Alaska is told in chapters set in this type face.

Alternating chapters, set in this type face, present the results of investigating the questions raised through Kennicott's autopsy as well as my experiences in reconstructing the story of the telegraph expedition.

At the conclusion of those fact-based chapters are my interpretations of what may have happened at certain times, possible explanations of otherwise unanswered questions.

The Autopsy
2001

Might it have been murder? Suicide, as some suggested? Or was it a natural death?

One hundred thirty years later, an autopsy would try to discover the truth.

The death of explorer, scientist, and naturalist Robert Kennicott made newspaper headlines in cities large and small throughout the United States because the reports of his exploits had captivated the country. During his 1859 trek through British Columbia, from Lake Superior to Fort Yukon, he wrote of exotic-sounding *rubbaboo* and *pemmican* from remote places such as Lake Athabasca and Slave River. He told of eight-man canoes daring river rapids, dogsleds speeding over mountains, and the sound of the human voice, eerie and echoing in sub-zero temperatures. But more important, Kennicott reported on the specimens of natural history that he collected for the Smithsonian Institution and other natural science museums.

The death of such a vital man shocked everyone, especially under the circumstances. Kennicott died at age thirty, alone, on the banks of the Yukon River, just below the Arctic Circle, near the Russian Fort Nulato, in 1866. The land he explored twice, Russian America, was purchased by the United States just ten months after he died. A later admirer believed, "Robert Kennicott is largely responsible for our purchase of Alaska. Without his knowledge of that mighty region, contained in a score of reports to the Smithsonian, we should never have known enough about Alaska to want it."[1]

Kennicott died five hundred river miles away from the nearest European settlement and months of dangerous ocean travel away from the United States. Yet, he was finally buried, in his third grave, at The Grove, his oak savannah home among the Illinois prairie grasses. Just as surprising, his body was in a sophisticated, state-of-the-art metal casket complete with a glass viewing plate in the face area. When he died, that kind of expensive casket was not routinely available in cities in the United States and certainly would not have been on hand at Nulato, a remote Russian fur-trading outpost.

Kennicott's death had been described at the time, but never explained. When the diary of George Adams, one of his fellow Alaskan explorers, was published in 1982, it included a journal Adams wrote fifty years after the events in the diary. In the journal, but not in the diary,

Adams said,

"Late that evening a white froth came from his mouth and then we realized that our commander Major Robert Kennicott had committed suicide by taking strychnine. We knew he had had strychnine to poison wild animals for their skins for the Smithsonian Institute at Washington. We could not find any of the strychnine about him or among his personal effects, and concluded that he had taken the poison and thrown the balance into the river, thinking that he could cover up the cause of his death and to further mystify us, he had made some meaningless marks on the sand nearby, a circle of a foot in diameter, placed his small pocket compass in the center, and made some lines from the compass towards the river, as if he was taking some kind of an observation." [2]

In addition, a comment made at the time of Kennicott's funeral was puzzling. William Stimpson, another Smithsonian scientist, wrote that when Kennicott's body arrived in Chicago, "We found that everything possible had been done; an air-tight metallic coffin prevented any perceptible decomposition...." [3] That seemed a remarkable statement for Stimpson to make since Kennicott had been dead for seven months before his body could have been placed in a metal casket. Yet, mourners could see Kennicott through the casket's glass face plate and Stimpson was obviously describing what they saw.

Did Kennicott's friends in the Yukon do something to preserve his body? Would it be possible to prove or disprove the suggestion of suicide? Now, a modern autopsy, using the most-accurate investigative tools, would try to answer the questions.

Kennicott's family home, The Grove, is a National Historic Landmark in Glenview,

The Kennicott home at The Grove, 1996.

Illinois northwest of Chicago, serving as both an education center and a nature center. Its director, Stephan Swanson, was going to move Kennicott's casket back to its original burial spot on the property and asked Dr. Douglas Owsley of the Smithsonian's National Museum of Natural History to conduct an autopsy at the same time to determine why Kennicott died. Owsley was willing because Kennicott was, in effect, a colleague who had grown up with the Smithsonian. The eighteen-year-old Kennicott began sending specimens to the six-year-old Institution because his contributions of animals, snakes, and insects from the prairie grasses were often new to Eastern scientists more familiar with woodland habitats. Then, too, Kennicott's fame-making three-year exploration into the middle of the North American continent, arranged through the Smithsonian, vastly increased its nature collections.

Now, Owsley's group of investigative scientists would try to determine the cause of Kennicott's too-early death.

Owsley, one of the nation's foremost forensic anthropologists, has identified victims of the Bosnian conflict and the Branch Davidian compound, and is a major contributor to the study of the nine- thousand-year-old Kenniwick Man. He called for the help of Dr. Arthur Aufderheide who established the field of paleopathology, reconstructing disease patterns by studying ancient mummies. Dr. Larry Cartmell would assist Aufderheide; Karin Bruwelheide, also of the Smithsonian, would assist Owsley.

Outside the large, yellow, log building at The Grove, it was a typical spring day in Chicago 2001. Above budding trees, mist hung from grey skies and sometimes coalesced into rain. Trilling red-winged blackbirds and a chorus of pond frogs competed with the thrum of trucks on a nearby expressway. Tiny blue scilla

On a foggy spring day, Kennicott's autopsy took place in the log building on the right. The log building across from it houses the education center and offices. A greenhouse is in the foreground.

flowers dotting the forest floor tried to look native rather than the escapees from the Kennicott family florist business they really were.

Inside the warehouse-type building, many bright lights hung from high rafters to give Chip Clark, award-winning Smithsonian photographer, on an equally tall ladder, the visibility he needed. The lights focused on Kennicott's still-closed casket, balanced on two sawhorses in the center of a large unobstructed area. Nearby, long folding tables, covered with sterile plastic, would hold items the scientists took from the casket. This autopsy would start with a full casket and would end with an empty one.

Everything would be removed, carefully, slowly, with many photographs and extensive descriptions of each step and every discovery. Autopsy is essentially a destructive art, allowing only one chance to see objects in position. Once something is removed, it really is not possible to put it back the way it was. Everything needs to be noted, commented on, written down immediately. Photographs are essential, both before and as the scientists work, because memory fades. Later, when questions come up, photographs often give the answer.

The scientists were primarily interested in Kennicott from an academic viewpoint. The twenty or so others in the

Left: Owsley describes the casket, its flanges sealed with lead and bolted together. In the head area, a metal plate covering a glass insert pivots aside to reveal the face of the deceased. Below: Steve Swanson, center, assesses the empty casket.

room, standing and whispering a discreet distance away, were more emotionally involved. Most of them were docents or program coordinators at The Grove's education center who had spent years learning about the Kennicotts, especially Robert. To be here, in this room, where his casket was about to be opened, was an opportunity they never expected. While they did not want to interfere with the scientific investigation, they did want to see as much as they could.

When the orange-brown rusted casket lid was lifted away, the circle of onlookers caught their breath with a soft "Ohhhh." Not in shock, but in appreciation of the dramatic remains. A gray cloth veiled Kennicott's body, toe to shoulder. The skull alone was visible, stained charcoal gray except for the bright white teeth with their multiple shiny gold and silver fillings.

The Smithsonian photographer took pictures. The Grove director took pictures. Before long, anyone with a camera had been invited to come close and, even leaning over the edge of the casket, took pictures from every angle. The crowded-out scientists were patiently indulgent. Just seeing the skull was enough to let them know there would not be much tissue remaining on which to test for chemicals or poisons. Because the casket's glass face plate had cracked, and because its rusted bottom had pinholes, air and water seeped into the casket and hastened decomposition, leaving primarily bones and artifacts for the scientists to examine.

When the cloth covering was removed, it was obvious Kennicott had been laid out. His jaw had been carefully held closed with a strip of white cloth knotted at the top of his head of dark wavy hair. His right arm was in the sleeve of his dark blue uniform coat with the double

The autopsy scientists: Larry Cartmell, Kari Bruwelheide, and Doug Owsley wear sterile plastic gloves and aprons as they begin their work. Art Aufderheide, not yet garbed, watches.

row of gold buttons, but his left arm was not. It was under the coat, resting across his abdomen. Kennicott had on not-very-worn gray wool uniform trousers over his long john underwear. The white, cotton, rib-topped socks on his feet — one with a hole in the toe — had not been covered by leather boots because there were no wooden boot heels in the casket. A light-weight, white, pleated, loosely fitting shirt covered his bare torso. On the upper arm of each shirt sleeve was stitched a narrow, grosgrain ribbon, now black but once colored. Intriguingly, each ribbon had an open knot tied into it. The ribbons did not circle the sleeves but reached about halfway around them. Kennicott's uniform cap was not in the casket, nor were his insignia on the coat's shoulders.

Once the autopsy began, The Grove staff could not believe their good fortune. They had expected to be kept behind ropes or relegated to far corners where they would have to stand on tiptoe to get even a glimpse. Instead, the scientists asked for their help and they eagerly agreed to do the most basic of chores. Set up more of the long, cafeteria-type tables? Sure. Find more buckets and containers? Right away. When the scientists needed a surface near them at the casket edge on which to put small items, one staffer grabbed a nearby empty black plastic deli tray, threw a sterile plastic apron over its scalloped edge and held it until it was full. She watched wide-eyed the whole time, knowing that nothing she had ever offered to do came close to this. Another staff member kept

saying, "This is sooo cool. They're letting us work! This is so coool."

That was the way it went throughout the examination of the remains. Everyone could ask questions, come up close to the action, or possibly perform as an assistant scientist for the day. When members of The Grove's board of directors stopped by, they were ushered as close as they cared to get and were told what was happening just then by the investigators. The scientists did not exactly stop working, but they explained at length what they were doing and what they were learning. As word of the welcoming atmosphere of the autopsy spread in the community, the circle of visitors observing the process constantly changed. A local patrolman in full uniform stood and watched for a long time, as intrigued as the school-children who also showed up.

A teenager in a Grove t-shirt at the front of the observing circle leaned over so far to see the skull Owsley was examining that his mom put her hands on

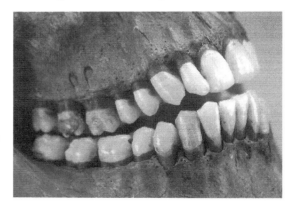

Kennicott's teeth show two oval facets caused by holding an abrasive pipe stem between the teeth. Kennicott smoked a clay pipe for about 10 years.

his shoulders to keep him from toppling. When invited to come closer, he walked up to the casket and interrupted Owsley's polite pleasantries to say, "Show me where his pipe went. I want to see the teeth where his pipe went." Owsley showed him the three pipe facets, teeth that had been worn away by an abrasive clay pipe stem so that an oval shape formed between two top teeth and two bottom teeth on both sides of the jaw. Entranced was the best word for the young man's expression. He was total attention, his eyes fixed on the skull and teeth. For long minutes, as far as he was concerned, there was clearly nothing in the large room but him, the skull, and Owsley's voice. When the rapt teen finally relaxed and smiled, he was given a pair of plastic gloves and asked to count the many small bones of the feet to be sure all of them had been found in Kennicott's socks.

The scientists appreciated help from all sources. When they looked puzzled on finding two small coat buttons, one at each clavicle midway between neck and shoulder, I suggested they might find a third one among the tangled hair and silk threads near the collar at the center back of the coat. I knew from my sewing projects that capes and hoods, like the one Kennicott wore in a photograph, are often attached with three buttons in those locations. The painstaking scientists would have found the button anyway, but my comment gave them a context for its presence.

My real job during the autopsy was to take notes on a laptop computer as the scientists worked. As a former English teacher with an interest in archaeology, I had never before come close to being involved in the scientific inquiry that is an autopsy. Several years earlier, I started working as a wordsmith for Owsley, offering to do what I had always done: make corrections and suggestions on essays and articles. My first task was to read innumerable reports describing the morphology, pathology, and taphonomy of bones. Two years of editing those repetitive, frankly eye-glazing, reports trained me to recognize and spell not only the bones of the body but also their possible injuries and diseases. When Owsley asked if I would record information during an autopsy scheduled at The Grove, I could not say yes fast enough. Now I could support him and his scientific team by recording their on-the-spot observations and comments. They described what they found, sometimes what it meant, sometimes questioned what they saw. I speed-typed phrases, abbreviations, and misspellings, going back later to fill out the sentences and get the right words to be turned into a running commentary on what happened during this autopsy.

For almost two full days, the scientists kept working, carefully dismantling the skeleton, looking for clues to Kennicott's death. Their operating premise was that Kennicott died of aortic valve stenosis, a calcification of the heart valve that, over time, stiffened so that blood could not flow. This condition often results from rheumatic fever, a common childhood disease in Kennicott's time. With luck, the stonelike valve, about the size and shape of a quarter coin, would be in the casket. It was not. Even though that did not necessarily disprove the rheumatic fever theory, the scientists decided to explore other possibilities.

The scientists did learn that, while Kennicott may have been a sickly child, he was never so sick that he stopped growing. Only one or two faint striations on his teeth and long bones show his growth was briefly arrested. His muscle attachment sites, while strong, did not indicate that he had spent years doing heavy lifting or manual labor. A small indention in his skull meant he had had a blow to the head at some early age, but it had healed, probably in his youth. No bones were broken or cracked, not even a rib or a finger, unusual in someone who spent months out of doors and primarily in the wild.

Based on his skeleton, Kennicott was right-handed and about five feet six inches tall. He also seems to have been in relatively good health when he died. The scientists took samples of his remains to test them for chemicals and heavy metals in hopes of getting clues to his health, but the autopsy itself ended with no firm conclusion as to the cause of Kennicott's death.

Perhaps checking the paper record — the letters Kennicott wrote, the reports from his last expedition, information from diaries — would answer some of the questions. Had childhood rheumatic fever left him with a malfunctioning heart? Might he have been murdered? Was the suggestion of suicide plausible? Did the men in the Yukon use special chemicals to preserve his body? For that matter, how did his body get back home? Where did the elegant casket come from? And, my own question: What is the explanation of those sleeve ribbons?

The investigation had to continue.

The Grove Archives 2002

Since the autopsy couldn't confirm the scientists' premise of a calcified valve, perhaps I could find records at his home to answer questions about Kennicott's health. Just how sickly was Kennicott as a child? Could his heart have been damaged by rheumatic fever?

Turning into the Kennicott property at The Grove from traffic-clogged Milwaukee Avenue in Glenview, Illinois, is a little like driving into an earlier century. A line of trees closed off the property so, with only a little imagination, highway tire noise became the wind. The long, curved, unpaved driveway could just as easily be bumped over by a carriage as a car. A broad lawn slopes gently up to the two-story, Gothic Revival home built in 1856 to replace the original ten-room log cabin of Kennicott's youth.

Beyond the house, the centuries blend. Much of the oak grove savannah, an oasis in the prairie, that attracted the Kennicotts when they moved from New Orleans in 1836, remains in its natural state. But within it now are new buildings built by The Grove to explain the Illinois ecosystem and the life of the Kennicotts.

One of the large, yellow, log buildings holds nature classrooms for local school children. Above the classrooms, a large loft provides office space for the small

Kennicott aged about 20. Undated photo.

staff and storage space for the Kennicott family records. Dedicated volunteers have painstakingly typed out the quantities of letters sent between family members, making my search for sickness a lot easier. Some letters are just notes of a line or two; others cover typed pages. But none of them offers specific information about Robert's health as a young child. Published accounts claim Robert was such a sickly child from his birth in 1835 that "it was doubtful whether he would long survive,"[1] but I couldn't find the proof in the letters.

I did get to know a flesh and blood

Kennicott family in which Robert morphed from the biographer's "intrepid explorer," and "dedicated naturalist" into a very real young man from an influential family that had already been in the United States for seven generations.

His father, John Kennicott, whom everyone called Ol' Doc, not only served as area physician, traveling on horseback to help the sick, but also as resident intellectual, gathering like-minded men for long conversations, and as commercial nurseryman, providing Northern Illinois farmers with trees, shrubs, and vines. Filling the plant orders often fell to his sons while he was in the state capitol working to establish, among other things, Land Grant College legislation. Letters show that Robert resented doing what he thought of as his father's work because it forced him to ignore his own as a scientist-naturalist. But he didn't mind contributing articles to the newsletter his father published for farmers.

Robert benefitted substantially from his father's extensive connections among the influential and educated. He studied with Dr. Philo R. Hoy, a leading ornithologist in Racine, Wisconsin, and with Jared Potter Kirtland, a preeminent scientist in Cleveland, Ohio. Ol' Doc's friendships throughout Illinois often resulted in work for Robert. On one of those jobs, for the Southern Illinois Railroad in 1855, Robert wrote several letters home describing a recurring problem: melancholy. At age nineteen, he felt extremely lonely, sad, worthless. He said he was working hard but, even when things went well, just felt he wasn't doing a good enough job; then, when things actually did go badly, he felt even worse. Robert asked for a prescription or advice, noting that his father and his uncle also seemed to regularly have such low-spirited, "blue" feelings.

In fact, a few years earlier, in 1853, Robert's father wrote that a "hypochondriacal and melancholic tendency runs through the whole family"[2] as he committed Robert's older brother, Charles, to a mental institution in Utica, N. Y. for six months. Ol' Doc added that for several previous years Charles "has been subject to ...attacks of mania preceded by depression of spirits and often brought on or at least aggravated by exposure to a hot sun."[3] Charles died in the Illinois State Hospital for the Insane, having been admitted three times between 1864 and his death in 1872.

Through these long-ago letters, I was beginning to feel like a close family friend, privy to information the Kennicotts might not have shared with everyone at the time.

A series of letters relates to the year-plus when Robert was very sick with an indefinable "ague," perhaps malaria. "The shakes" began in June 1855 when Robert was working in southern Illinois. He dosed himself with quinine and came home to recover. Robert condensed the events of six months in a January 1856 letter: "Since last July no two successive weeks have passed in which I have not had the fever upon me. You may suppose I have no energy left either bodily or mental. I spent about two months in Chicago trying to attend College during which time I probably went to the lectures twenty days in all. I have given it up in despair and am now at home on an allowance of seven grams of quinine daily .... I fear I shall not be able to do much before summer. I shall thus have lost nearly a year."[4]

During that time, Robert's mother, Mary, wrote Ol' Doc, who was traveling, about his son's condition and the medicines she'd given. "I gave Bob quinine Sunday evening as you directed but he was very sick all day Monday... I have given him a teaspoon full of rhubarb and jalap – one part jalap and three parts rhubarb. About a half hour after he took it a diarrhea came on...if I think it is operating too much I will give him something to check it and will give him quinine this afternoon and early in the morning."[5] Obviously, Robert's mother was familiar with the prescriptives and dosages of the standard medicine chest. Rhubarb was routinely used as a laxative; jalap was the powdered root of a morning glory, Ipomoea Purga, used as a purgative. It wouldn't have been surprising to find

The Kennicott home at The Grove, c. 1860s. When it was built, 20-year-old Kennicott had already begun his scientific career and rarely lived in his family's home.

she'd tucked those into a travel package for her son.

Instead, the family sent their explorer son strychnine.

A packing list of supplies sent to Robert for his 1858 specimen-collecting exploration into British America showed twenty-one bottles of strychnine divided among several boxes packed in Chicago. The poison would not only kill large animals but would also help to preserve them as specimens. So strychnine as a scientific supply was not unexpected. The surprise came in a separate box. Along with such personal items as toothbrushes were "2 gal. good old Scotch whiskey" and "1 oz. of strychnine."[6] Easy enough to account for the whiskey; they believed alcohol prevented disease. Why would they send strychnine?

There would have been no difference between the strychnine packed in Chicago and that packed by the family. Strychnine comes in one form: a small crystal similar to salt or sugar. It comes in one strength; in one bitter flavor. Was the family showing their support for his occupation by contributing a scientific necessity? But just one ounce of it? That quantity sounds more like a medicine. In 1857 a patient of Ol' Doc's was taking strychnine to build robust strength. Would Robert's doctor-father have prescribed strychnine for his son? If so, what ailment was the medicine designed to help? Was this strychnine somehow related to the strychnine Robert carried in Russian America?

What did happen on that Western Union expedition?

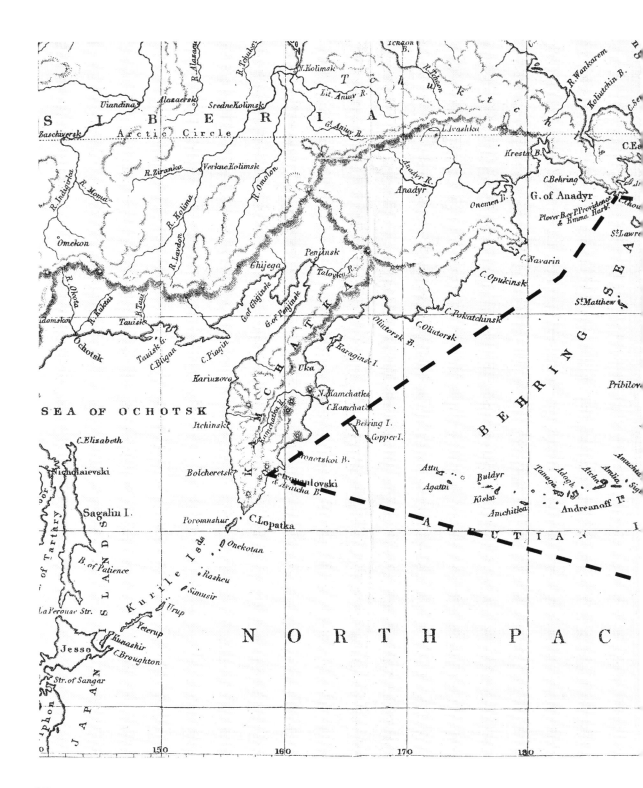

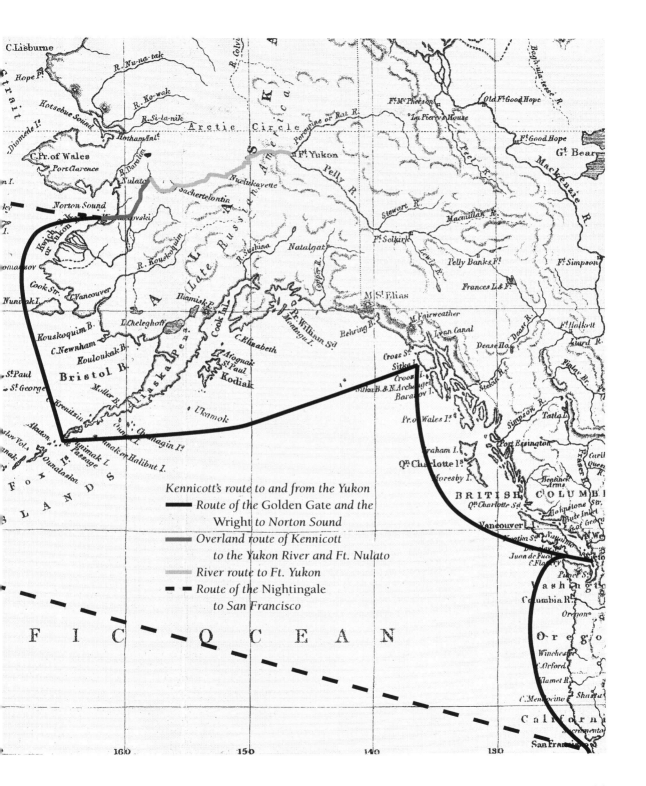

Kennicott's route to and from the Yukon

—— Route of the *Golden Gate* and the
    Wright to Norton Sound

—— Overland route of Kennicott
    to the Yukon River and Ft. Nulato

—— River route to Ft. Yukon

– – Route of the *Nightingale*
    to San Francisco

Personnel

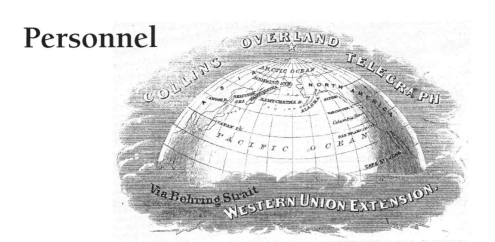

IN CHICAGO

William **Stimpson**, Smithsonian scientist appointed Director of the Chicago Academy of Science in Kennicott's absence

George **Walker**, president of the Chicago Academy of Sciences

IN WASHINGTON, DC

Spencer Fullerton **Baird**, Assistant Secretary (vice-president) of the Smithsonian Institution

Joseph **Henry**, Secretary (president) of the Smithsonian Institution

---

IN THE YUKON

Colonel Charles S. **Bulkley**, in charge of the total Western Union telegraph operation in both America and Russia

Charles **Scammon**, commander of the *Nightingale*, supporter of the Scientific Corps

Under William **Ennis**, appointed by Kennicott as his second in command; in charge of exploring the northern area of Norton Sound

  Oscar **Bendeleben**, close Yukon friend of Kennicott

  Jay **Chappel**

  Richard **Cotter**, at Nulato

  Thomas **Dennison**

  Joseph **Dyer**, at Nulato

Under Robert **Kennicott**, in charge of the whole exploration of Russian America, particularly the Yukon River

  George **Adams**, hired by Kennicott in San Francisco; diarist; at Nulato

  Henry **Bannister**, Scientific Corps member; stationed at Fort St. Michael's; diarist

  William **Dall**, Scientific Corps member; stationed in San Francisco; diarist

  Frank **Ketchum**, appointed by Kennicott to continue explorations; at Nulato

  Michael **Lebarge**, at Nulato

  Simon Evan **Lukine**, Russian-native guide; at Nulato

  Charles **Pease**, Scientific Corps member; Kennicott's boyhood friend; at Nulato

  Frederick **Smith**, hired by Kennicott in San Francisco; diarist; at Nulato

Chicago 1864

So snowblind that he could only stumble along the hillside, Robert Kennicott finally gave in. The sun-softened snow clung to his snowshoes making every footstep a weight-lifting, muscle-straining effort. What was worse, his watched stopped. Now he could not count his footsteps per minute, multiply by the length of his stride and how long he had been walking, to approximate how far he had traveled. Was he close to the fort, or not? In the snowscape around him, everything, and nothing, looked familiar. He took his one blanket, tried to forget how long it had been since he had finished the last of his rations, and rolled up to sleep the heat of the day away. When the snow iced over in the night's freezing temperatures, making snowshoeing easier, he would continue his trek.

Here he was, in the Yukon, in the winter, exactly where he had tried so hard not to be. But he could not quit; he had given his word. To the Smithsonian Institution and the Chicago Academy of Sciences that hoped he would provide specimens of plants and animals never before seen in the United States. To the Western Union Company that wanted him to find a good path for their projected overland telegraph line.

The new Western Union economic adventure would make all of the telegraph company's previous expansion plans seem puny. This time, it would wire the continents together. Ambitious competitors had previously decided to connect America with western Europe by laying telegraph wire hundreds of miles under the Atlantic Ocean. Western Union's equally audacious plan, begun in 1864, would go in the opposite direction, over land, from western America through eastern Europe.

Western Union had already united the nation by wire in 1861, so it was eager to expand to Europe. The plan was the brainchild of entrepreneur Perry McDonough Collins who received permission from the Czar of Russia to cross Russian America (now Alaska), from the Queen of England to cross British America (now Canada), and from the Congress of the United States to use land on the west coast. Then he joined his enterprise to Western Union. In Collins's plan, the telegraph would begin on the United States's west coast, make its way inland north to the Yukon River, follow that river west until it bent too far south, find a more direct path to the coast, cross the Bering Strait, travel the Russian coast south to the Amur River, follow the Amur into Siberia and then go on to St. Petersburg. Since Collins planned to go over land, using the narrowest possible connection point between the two continents, his wire would go under water for only the short distance of the Bering Strait.

Collins's plan sounded no more impossible than had fellow entrepreneur Cyrus Field's plan to lay telegraph cable completely under water from Ireland to Newfoundland. And Field had succeeded, if briefly. When the transatlantic cable failed in 1858, his backers accused him of fraud. Now, in 1864, the war between North and South that had discouraged investors seemed to be winding down; Field was raising money for another underwater attempt; and an overland telegraph, even in the Far North, attracted supporters eager to be part of the newest promise of fortune.

The telegraph was by far the fastest method of communication available. A letter sent between the continents took almost two weeks to arrive as sailing ships fought the ocean. A letter sent over half the American continent, between Chicago and Washington, was speedily delivered in about four days. In just three days, a telegram could be delivered across the whole continent, between San Francisco and Washington.

The 1838 invention of the telegraph is usually credited to Samuel B. Morse, the man who grasped the commercial possibilities of electrically transmitted sound. Others worked with electric current much earlier and in 1830, Joseph Henry, later the first Secretary of the Smithsonian Institution, sent an electric current over one

A telegraph key, when tapped, makes and breaks an electric circuit causing a clicking sound. Operators spell out each word of a message.

mile of wire to activate at its end an electromagnet that caused a bell to strike. Causing such movement over long distances became the functional core of the telegraph. Telegraph operators tapped a single key that looked like a typewriter key, making and breaking an electrical contact. The resulting pulse of electricity, carried over miles of wire, moved a distant key, making a clicking sound. Morse then combined a system of long and short pulses into a code for the letters of the alphabet so that words could be spelled out. Morse code was so successful that years later two of the simplest sounds, for letters S (three short pulses) and O (three long pulses), became the international distress signal, SOS. A trained telegraph operator could send between forty and fifty words per minute, from one telegraph office to another.

Admittedly, Field's transatlantic cable was not that fast. It took two minutes for one character of Morse code to be transmitted across the ocean; the first message from England was received over sixteen hours. Western Union, confident that it would be able to offer better service, began collecting the resources it would need to construct a telegraph line just below the Arctic Circle. Kennicott was one of the resources.

Kennicott was the only person in the United States who had lived in the Arctic. He had traveled through the mountains and snows of Russian America, had written clear and even entertaining descriptions of his experiences there, and was respected for his unbiased observations. Before his detailed reports of his explorations, all information about conditions in the Far North came from ship-based observations of the coast; some of those who reported on the terrain had not even stepped ashore. Kennicott, from 1858 to 1862, conducted a one-man expedition to collect specimens of natural history from the center of the American continent, an area whose plants, animals, and geology were almost completely unknown to science. Kennicott worked his way north and west through British America from Lake Superior at the border of the United States to Fort Mackenzie in the north. Then, in winter 1861, with a visa from the Czar written in Cyrillic and English, he crossed the western mountains to reach the British Fort Yukon in Russian American territory. Kennicott knew about the Arctic weather and terrain not just from personal experience but, more important to Western Union's plans, from being inland. With his background of dogsleds for travel, pemmican for food, and natives for companions, Kenni-

Morse Code

A	● —
B	— ● ● ●
C	— ● — ●
D	— ● ●
E	●
F	● ● — ●
G	— — ●
H	● ● ● ●
I	● ●
J	● — — —
K	— ● —
L	● — ● ●
M	— —
N	— ●
O	— — —
P	● — — ●
Q	— — ● —
R	● — ●
S	● ● ●
T	—
U	● ● —
V	● ● ● —
W	● — —
X	— ● ● —
Y	— ● — —
Z	— — ● ●
1	● — — — —
2	● ● — — —
3	● ● ● — —
4	● ● ● ● —
5	● ● ● ● ●
6	— ● ● ● ●
7	— — ● ● ●
8	— — — ● ●
9	— — — — ●
0	— — — — —

Spencer Fullerton Baird, c. 1860s

cott would be invaluable to Western Union's expedition.

The connection between Kennicott and Western Union was Spencer Fullerton Baird, the first Assistant Secretary of the young Smithsonian Institution. Baird, determined to make the Smithsonian a repository of as much information as possible, began corresponding with the budding prairie scientist Kennicott in 1853. Baird encouraged Kennicott to send natural history specimens from his unknown-to-science environment in the West, as Illinois was then called. Baird taught Kennicott the finer points of zoology at the Smithsonian in 1857, and, recognizing his potential, organized the financial backing for his three-year exploration of British America.

Baird, working within sight of the Capitol, presumably kept track of events in Congress. He would have known the views of Charles Sumner, chairman of the Senate Committee on Foreign Relations, who ardently supported the idea that the United States had a Manifest Destiny to control the whole of North America. When Baird learned that Western Union needed information about part of that destiny, Russian America and the Yukon, he offered the services of the Smithsonian Institution and pressed for Kennicott's cooperation.

When Baird encouraged him to help Western Union with their telegraph expedition, Kennicott already had more than enough to do. From his recent trek through British America to Fort Yukon, he had sent back hundreds of specimens of the natural world. Those rare and unusual specimens were destined for the financial backers of the trip: the Smithsonian Institution, the University of Michigan, and most important to him, the Chicago Academy of Sciences. Now, in 1864, Kennicott was fully engrossed in his own personal enterprise: building on those specimens to turn the little-known Chicago Academy into a Smithsonian of the West. His grand vision would "make Chicago the great centre of Science in the west — as it is now of wealth and of commercial intellect and energy — so that great philosophers may find here an inviting house."[1] Kennicott started invigorating the Academy in 1862, shortly after returning from his trek, by promoting its potential and by ceaseless fundraising among Chicago's businessmen. His task was made slightly easier because his name was familiar. The Kennicott family's horticultural business west of the city was well known in Chicago; Kennicott's relatives were dentists and doctors in the city.

His father was particularly respected as an intelligent and influential contributor to the growth of the state, and Kennicott's personal exploits in science were highly regarded. But more, his often bright and enthusiastic personality made him a congenial addition to social groups, increasing the willingness of contacts to open their purses. After two successful years accumulating both money and supporters, he now spent all of his days and most of his evenings totally focused on the physical building of the Academy. He devised a floor plan; designed display cases; stuffed, mounted and labeled specimens. He knew he could do it because he had previously established a small nature museum at Northwestern University in nearby Evanston.

On this much larger project, a major museum, Kennicott, who preferred working alone, looked for help. He asked his young Northwestern assistant, Henry Bannister, to pitch in now at the Academy. He hired an experienced taxidermist, Ferdinand Bischoff from downstate Illinois. A young scientist trained at Harvard, William Healey Dall, who was working in Chicago as a personal secretary, devoted evenings and weekends to the Academy. Kennicott supervised them all, in addition to the other men working on the building itself, and he gratefully accepted the drop-in help of many who stopped by to see the building's progress.

To all of those concerns on Kennicott's mind, Baird urged adding the Western Union expedition. Initially, Kennicott refused to become involved but finally agreed to tell the expedition planners what he knew about the Arctic. At Baird's insistence, he met several times over the summer of 1864 with the company's officers and board members in Rochester, NY. Baird, too, met with Western Union that summer and the contributions of both Baird and Kennicott were substantial. "[Kennicott] spent nearly the whole day at the Telegraph Office. His views throughout coincided with yours [Baird's], and [Board president] Mr. Sibley, who had been deeply impressed by your statements, became thoroughly converted. ...[Kennicott] described a route which Mr. Sibley said would save more than half the calculated expense.... On the region west of the Rocky Mountains concerning which we are to inquire, K. poured very cold water...."[2]

Kennicott suggested running the telegraph line through British America taking basically the same route he had used to reach Fort Yukon. He appreciated that such a route would be over familiar

Kennicott, c. 1860s

river valleys and foot paths long used by the trappers and traders of the Hudson's Bay Company. Throughout Kennicott's three-year trek, he essentially was handed on from one British fort to the next following the extensive routes of the fur trade. His trek, calculated as 2500 straight-line miles but actually many hundreds of miles longer over hills, around rapids, and through forests, was difficult enough even with the traders' help. Kennicott could attest that a coastal route through unknown and mountainous terrain would be difficult to impossible.

The Western Union Board finally rejected both the coastal and the central routes but agreed on another suggestion, taking the line north from Vancouver between the Coastal Mountains and the Rocky Mountains to the Yukon River and from there west to the Bering Strait. Kennicott, who had not wanted to join the expedition because he thought of himself as a naturalist not an explorer, now reconsidered. He was elated with the informal proposal Western Union made him, writing Baird excitedly, "I was to get 50 shares of stock for what I've already done. That in the event of my going with the Exped. I should have 100 additional shares...and receive $100 per month and all expenses paid."[3]

Other factors besides the money he could use for the Academy may have helped change Kennicott's mind. He had been widely and highly praised for his scientific work, particularly for the fine collections of natural history he made in British America and contributed to respected museums. He now recognized he could do as much in Russian America because the commander of the expedition assured Baird, "it is the intention to have a thorough survey of the country, which will furnish more definite and reliable information than any heretofore published."[4] In helping Western Union, Kennicott could expand and extend his reputation not just within science but in the general public by reporting on unknown areas of the continent: Norton Sound and the Yukon River.

Improving on this new vision, Kennicott bargained to include a Scientific Corps in the expedition. Collecting scientific data while exploring new lands was an established tradition that would benefit both Western Union and Kennicott. He would multiply the amount of information and specimens that could be collected; the company would gain the prestige of increasing knowledge while operating a profit-making enterprise. It would cost the company very little because Kennicott offered to split his own salary among six young scientists, each a specialist in a different field. Western Union agreed; the handpicked scientists could collect natural history specimens as long as they also did what they could to help the expedition when needed.

In December 1864, Kennicott formally signed on with the Collins Overland Telegraph, Western Union Extension.

Before Kennicott could leave, he needed to ready the Chicago Academy for its opening, planned for spring. Throughout the next months, he worked feverishly. Earlier that November, he lamented to Baird, "I've got carpenter and case-maker on the brain and there is now bad indications of its affecting the liver — only Blue Mass [a mercury-based pill] and the thought of Norton Sound zoology can keep me from getting discouraged."[5] Under this pressure, the scientists worked many nights on specimens and exhibits until midnight; Kennicott even lived at the Academy. He told Baird in January, "As the time draws near when I must leave I have such an overwhelming sense of the am't. of work I must leave unfinished that I am hardly aware whether I stand on my head or my heels."[6] On January 19, 1865, Dall, Bannister and others worked late at the Academy. Dall noted in his diary, "We get through considerable work and have a pleasant evening. K. had an attack of the vertigo."[7] Whatever Dall meant by 'vertigo,' whether dizziness or fainting, Kennicott's attack was obviously strong enough or long enough for Dall to make note of it hours later as he ended his day.

A few weeks later, fire destroyed the top floor of the Smithsonian Castle in Washington, consuming hundreds of painstakingly collected specimens. Kennicott offered to quit the telegraph expedition to replace the losses, but Baird refused his help knowing that new specimens from an unexplored country would be more valuable to science. Kennicott continued his work at the Academy but was gone the month of February, visiting a circuit of museums in Boston, New York, Philadelphia, Baltimore, and Washington, seeing all the scientific men he could. As he explained to Baird, he "crowded the work of months into weeks and almost into days"[8] and acknowledged, "I'm working double hard now and am pretty well played out."[9]

There was still one more problem to solve: the administration of the Academy in Kennicott's absence. At last, with Baird's prodding, Kennicott's friend from Smithsonian days, William Stimpson, agreed to take over until Kennicott's return. Stimpson had helped the Western Union expedition already by organizing the information he had collected in 1852, when he was asked by Baird to travel to the North Pacific and the Bering Strait. Although this North Pacific Exploring Expedition mapped and collected only along the coast, the information it brought back was far more extensive than had previously been available. Stimpson was at the Smithsonian, preparing his collection, when Kennicott arrived in 1857 and the two men became fast friends. Stimpson rented a cottage for the two of them and other young Smithsonian interns, who informally called themselves the Megatherium, after an extinct giant sloth whose fossilized skeleton was famously studied by Charles Darwin. The men worked diligently during the day, but kept their evening hours for socializing. As Kennicott described the group, "It is [at] five o'clock, when the Megatherium takes its prey [at dinner], that the most interesting characters [characteristics] of the animal are seen. Then it roars with delight and makes up for the hard work of the day by much fun and conduction [conversation]..."[10] Stimpson asserted that "Kennicott's voice was ever the most cheery, his tale the freshest, and his song the blithest."[11] Now, Stimpson would hold his friend Kennicott's place in Chicago, restoring it to him at the end of the expedition.

Kennicott returned to Chicago from his Eastern museum-hopping on March 5 and waited for Stimpson to arrive for a briefing. By March 9, 1865, Kennicott had wound up his affairs in Chicago. He then left for Washington to join the Scientific Corps for ten days at the Smithsonian Castle, to share and absorb information about the region they were to explore.

Smithsonian Institution Archives 2001–2008

After the inconclusive autopsy, Owsley asked if I would like to "read some papers" about Kennicott at the Smithsonian Archives. It sounded like the perfect assignment: I live only twenty minutes by subway from the Smithsonian and Kennicott's papers were kept right there in the Arts and Industries building on the Mall. I could drop in any day I wanted and stay as long as I liked, whereas most researchers have to request their items from off-site storage days in advance and plan their lives accordingly.

It did seem strange to do research in Washington knowing that Kennicott lived and worked primarily in Chicago. Why wasn't all the information available in Chicago? Answer: The Chicago Fire. What Mrs. O'Leary's cow started in 1871 nearly finished off the city and significantly damaged the Chicago Academy of Sciences. In wooden Chicago, the Academy had responsibly built a fire-resistant stone building for its specimens and stored its paper records in a metal, fireproof safe. But when the fire had burned past and the directors confidently went to check on their building, they found the fire had weakened the structure to the point that the heavy front pediment had crashed to the basement, directly on top of the safe. All the papers in the burst-open safe were carbon flakes. Any reports, journals,

letters, or records of Kennicott floated in the wind. Professor Baird, with whom Kennicott had worked at the Smithsonian and with whom he had corresponded for years, had kept those letters, as well as information from the Western Union Telegraph Expedition. All were in the Smithsonian Institution Archives. Research results couldn't be perfect, but might be enough.

When I started, in 2001, the offices and reading room of the Archives were housed in a magnificent red brick building constructed in 1881 just east of the Smithsonian Castle right in the center of the Mall. It was built to hold all the exhibits of the Smithsonian in a high-ceilinged cross-plan structure with a central rotunda. But, as new museums were built to showcase the Institution's growing collections, the original museum building declined and decayed. When I first walked in, a large circular fountain still sparkled at the central crossing of the four main halls and the Horticulture Department still surrounded the splashing water with seasonal flowers. Few visitors came into the building. At one point, a store opened, selling items from all the other museums. Then it closed. A small deli opened. Then it closed. Once, there was a splendid orchid exhibit. Then, nothing. The building closed to the public in 2005.

All those years, I walked to the central

crossing where a set of stairs in each corner led up, each closed by a velvet-covered rope clasped by a brass hook to a brass loop in the wall. I opened only the stair rope nearest the Archives. The balcony hallway around the second floor held many doorways but I only used the doorway to the Archives. A makeshift plywood canopy, evidently designed to protect visitors from falling plaster caused by a leaky skylight, covered the entrance. Entering Archives to examine the strange land of the past began with entering a short, sort-of tunnel reminding me of the wardrobe into the wonderland of Narnia.

Opening the Archives door changed my fictional scene to something out of Dickens. In the small outer office, behind an old, scarred, wood desk, sat an older woman. She directed me to hang my coat on the brass hooks of a tall, gorgeous, carved oak cloak stand complete with a center beveled mirror and a base divided into little cubes for umbrellas and canes. Perfect. I signed in on a slant-top table straight out of Scrooge's office.

I looked Dickensian as well, as I sat in the small, dark-paneled, windowless reading room with my pencil and paper. Other researchers typed notes into their laptop computers, but my retro method asserted that what I was doing was a simple, short-term project. There was no point in gearing up. Many months later, when it became clear I was well into a complicated, long-term project, I had so many pencil notes it didn't seem reasonable to transfer everything to a computer. I was trapped in Dickens's century.

Various very patient archivists were on call to help bewildered researchers. Who would have guessed that information about Kennicott could be found not only under his name but also under Baird, Bannister, and Bulkley, with the rest of the alphabet yet to search? The enormity of "reading some papers" began to register.

Archivists loaded the carefully labeled gray file boxes I asked for onto carts and wheeled them to my library table. Flipped open, the boxes held buff file folders, also carefully labeled and numbered, containing hand-written letters, typed reports, photographs, and drawings. It was a treasure trove of information about Kennicott from his first year with the Smithsonian to his last. From the Archives I would learn most of what I needed to know. The only thing that kept me from blissful absorption in all this information was the reading room temperature: probably one degree above freezing, summer and winter. If things last longer when they're chilled, I added years to my life.

Just as I was wrapping up my research, the office closed completely in 2006 in order to move. It reopened in a brand new office-type building nearby but off the Mall. In the new space, daylight poured through walls of glass onto light-colored reading tables containing multiple outlets for personal computers. A full row of public computers faced the windows, and multiple machines would copy different types and sizes of materials.

As grateful as I was for the new conveniences, there was an appeal to that velvet rope at the foot of the stairs and that protective tunnel into the past that I missed.

Spring 1865

When the Scientific Corps members met at the Smithsonian, some of them were already friends because Kennicott relied heavily on people he knew personally, men he could count on to observe acutely and record accurately their experiences.

When Kennicott asked Bannister, his meticulous museum assistant, to come, Bannister wrote his parents for permission, assuring them, "I don't see that there is any danger to be feared and the time will not be much, only nine or ten months, a year at the most, and it certainly will not be lost."[1] Because Bannister's parents were reluctant to give their only son permission, Kennicott wrote Professor Bannister at Northwestern University to urge them to let Henry go, saying it would be more beneficial to him than a year of schooling. They finally agreed.

Henry Martyn Bannister: Age 20; trained under Baird and Kennicott

Dall was harder to sell. From his evening hours at the Academy, he was used to Kennicott's "boyish enthusiasm" and "somewhat incoherent manner of speaking," but he could not understand the expedition. To him, the expedition did not just seem "somewhat indefinite in plan" but "so wrapped in mystery that I shall not regard it, until I can find out the particulars."[2] When Dall lost his secretarial position and despite letters of recommendation could not find another, he was more receptive. In February 1865, during his Eastern museums trip, Kennicott wrote in almost incoherent haste on Smithsonian letterhead to Dall, who had moved into Kennicott's rooms at the Academy. Kennicott urged him to join the Scientific Corps, but explained that the Western Union directors could not officially recognize the group; it was a special arrangement with the expedition's commander. At that point, winter was ebbing and spring in Chicago had few charms for Dall who saw it as "mud unfathomable and slop inconceivable, except to an inhabitant,"[3] a dark opinion perhaps further colored by his unemployment. Philosophically, he observed, "This world is all chance and I stand as good a chance [to find a job] two years from now as now. ...I had better go North."[4]

William Healey Dall: Age 19; a marine biologist trained by Harvard's prominent ichthyologist and Darwin supporter, Louis Agassiz

Charles Pease, Jr.: Age 30; Kennicott's boyhood friend with some scientific training

George W. Maynard: Age 22; an artist from Washington, DC who volunteered

Charles Pease, Jr., the only man not directly associated with science, may have been added to the group for Kennicott's personal reasons. Pease was a boyhood friend of Kennicott's from the year when they both studied with Pease's noted naturalist grandfather, Kirtland. Pease, now an Ohio businessman involved in a short-line railroad to a local vacation spot, was married with children and rumored to drink too much. But he knew about boats and boating and would be in charge of the steamer Kennicott had convinced Western Union to supply.

To document this extraordinary expedition, the group needed an artist. Even though photographs were being taken, the cumbersome and expensive equipment required for photography limited its use. The artist son of a Baird family friend, George Maynard, volunteered.

Baird also recommended Joseph Trimble Rothrock, the only scientist not known to Kennicott. The combination of these two scientists brought some of the issues of the bloody Civil War directly into the expedition. Rothrock depended heavily on a cane because he was recuperating from a severe leg wound received while a Union cavalry captain on the Fredericksburg battlefield. Only because of his war wound was he available for the Scientific Corps. Able-bodied Kennicott never joined the army. Years earlier, in 1862, Kennicott heard about the war when he was at Fort Yukon and, infuriated by the idea of a split in the nation, he hurried home from his trek determined to join the Union Army. At the start of the conflict, his father commented that it was too bad Robert was not in Illinois because, with his engaging personality, he would have been able to raise a regiment in no time and take his place at the head of it. A brother and a sister were already serving the Union in the war. However, when Kennicott returned, his friends talked him out of volunteering, convincing him he could better serve his country by contributing scientific information about it.

Kennicott was finally drafted in September 1864, just as he was planning for the telegraph expedition. "Good joke, eh?" he wrote Baird ironically and worried that he would have to go.[5] The Chicago Academy offered to buy a substitute for him, a legal and generally accepted option available to anyone. Instead, he arranged for an advance on his salary from the Academy and for some loans from friends in order to purchase a substitute himself.

Now Kennicott and Rothrock, non-soldier and wounded soldier, would be together in Washington where the tents of Union soldiers covered available open spaces and where Walt Whitman tended the wounded in the Patent Building not far from the Smithsonian where the Scientific Corps gathered to study.

Bischoff, the Chicago Academy's taxidermist from Peoria, Illinois, quickly signed on as did Henry Wood Elliott, a young scientist Kennicott mentored at the Smithsonian.

All of the young men in Kennicott's Scientific Corps were very promising scientists. With the possible exception of Pease, all reflected the stereotype of a scholar: slightly built, intensely focused, and from learned families. Kennicott's father was a doctor; Bannister's father a professor of languages at a seminary; Dall's father a missionary in India; Rothrock's father a doctor. Even so, as far as the expedition was concerned, their major characteristics only needed to be the "muscle and will sufficient for the occasion."[6] Many of the naturalists had, of course, spent time out of doors collecting specimens but Kennicott had "explored" in the sense of depending on his own resourcefulness for a long period of time. He alone had experienced the rigors of winter in the Far North.

For ten days at the Smithsonian, they all got to know each other and learned as much as was available about Russian America and the Yukon River. Other Western Union expedition members had come to the Smithsonian before them. When the head of the whole expedition "arrived in New York to assume the work of constructing this line, he found his first light in consultation with these gentlemen [Kennicott and Baird.] They aided him in the construction of his maps, from them he derived the necessary information in respect to preparation of stores, and at Washington he was introduced by Prof. Baird to the latest results of Russian exploration, translated for his purpose into English, and illustrated with photograph copies of drawings."[7] The assistant engineer of the Western Union team and authority on the telegraph came to the Smithsonian for the latest and most reliable Russian, British, and American information from which he drafted a map of the proposed route of the Western Union extension to the Collins Overland Telegraph.

Based on all this planning, Kennicott anticipated being in the Arctic by late spring, in time for the nesting season that would provide the eggs and other important information about birds observed only as adults in the temperate zones. Expecting to accomplish their goals during long Arctic summer days, Bannister confi-

Joseph Trimble Rothrock: Age 26; a botanist trained by Harvard's Asa Gray, the most important botanist of the nineteenth century

Henry Wood Elliott: Age 19; a Smithsonian trained naturalist and amateur artist

dently wrote his concerned parents, "My outfit will be very simple as I shall want nothing more than a suit of strong rough clothes like corduroys, a pair of heavy boots and perhaps a knapsack."[8]

As the Scientific Corps left the East on March 21, 1865, to join the expedition forming in San Francisco, Smithsonian Secretary Henry wrote a friend, "We had quite a clearing out at the Institution yesterday. Kennicott and five men left for Russian America to join the telegraph company....They are all full of energy, enthusiasm and excitement. I fear however that they will not be able to do as much in the way of Natural History as they anticipate because the essential object of the expedition is the exploration and establishment of the telegraph line and the conditions will scarcely allow any other object to interfere with this."[9]

To get from the East Coast of the United States to the West Coast, the Scientific Corps had several equally onerous options. While railroad lines crisscrossed the East and penetrated the country beyond Chicago, the Golden Spike uniting the coasts by rail was not driven until 1869; it was not possible for the Scientific Corps to take a train to San Francisco. Stage coaches required multiple stops and many transfers of baggage to reach the coast through warring Indian country. Routes by ship were more reliable but still lengthy and dangerous. Freight and passengers could sail down the long coasts of North and South America, around the ship-wrecking Cape Horn, and back up the two coasts. Or, passengers could take a ship as far as the isthmus between North and South America, disembark and make their way overland through a string of rivers and lakes to the opposite coast where they could embark on another ship to their destination. The Scientific Corps, using this option, left from New York for the Isthmus of Panama aboard the paddle-wheel steamer *Golden Rule*.

Even before boarding, Kennicott immediately employed those personal qualities that had helped him accomplish so much. Through cajoling, humouring, pleading, and in Dall's words, "a little judicious wire-pulling," Kennicott managed to get his Corps good staterooms instead of the standing berths the economical Western Union had reserved for them.[10]

One evening at dinner on the steamer, Charlie Pease asked a waiter, "Wasn't this vessel in dry dock...?" When the waiter answered, "Yes," Pease deadpanned, "Did she roll much?" and brought down the house with his image of a ship out of water still rocking from side to side.[11] Pease was able to joke about the major problem with the ship, but others did not find the constant rolling very funny. The *Golden Rule* was, as the non-seaman Bannister observed, "a very lively vessel in a sea; ...the hull is so cut away fore and aft for the sake of speed that she can hardly lie still at the wharf." [12] Bannister returned to bed seasick the very first day; Elliott followed him shortly. Dall put himself on an "anti-Jonah diet" of hard tack and ham, trying to calm his stomach. Then the weather turned stormy and almost everyone became seasick.

On top of everything, the passengers harbored a generalized anxiety about the war. It was not over, they were steaming south along the coast of Confederate States, and they had no new information about conditions in the conflict. When the passengers spotted a boat near Charleston, South Carolina, rumors started that it was a gunboat and people immediately concluded it was a feared rebel pirate ship, the *Shenandoah*. After tense minutes, passengers could see it was not, and they steamed on safely.

In the ten days it took to reach Nicaragua, the scientists made careful notes of what they saw: flying fish, pods of dolphin, types of seaweed. Even so, they had time on their hands. Pease stared at the Biblical picture of Rebecca and Isaac on his cabin wall, perhaps thinking of his own wife and family. Elliott amused himself and the other passengers by drawing caricatures. Kennicott, after the months of exertion and anxiety preparing for the trip, became "semi-comatose ... too lazy to get seasick."[13] Still, he was discovering which other passengers were interested in natural history, which had already collected specimens for their own use, which might be diligent enough to collect for the Smithsonian. It seemed he hoped to repeat his successful recruitment of the trappers he met on his trek through British America.

Kennicott's rapport with the trappers of the Hudson's Bay Company during his three years in their company brought long-term dividends to the Smithsonian. Many of those trappers and traders were self-trained naturalists, close observers of animal behaviors and habitats, who appreciated being taught by Kennicott how to professionally prepare specimens that they then sent to the Smithsonian. This was a major coup for American science because until then specimens had been sent to England. Even as Kennicott steamed toward South America, Baird was sending preservation supplies to Kennicott's friends in northern America and receiving

Kennicott, c. 1862, posed in the French trapper clothing he wore on his 1859 expedition through British America to Fort Yukon.

specimens in return. Kennicott was eager to replicate that success.

Kennicott's three years in British America form the core of his lifework and his contributions to science in these years cannot be over-emphasized. The Smithsonian credits 282 birds and 230 mammals to Kennicott during this period. Even those large numbers do not include Kennicott's contributions to other specimen categories such as snakes, amphibians, fish, and insects. Kennicott's contributions go beyond specimens of nature to include examples of native clothing, pipes, and headdresses. A quick learner with a good ear, he was able to converse with many of the tribes after a relatively short time. He worked with the many official translators for the tribes to create and send to Baird extensive dictionaries of their languages, often the first written records of their speech.

In truth, Kennicott collected and sent back everything of interest that he saw along his voyage: a rock from Great Slave Lake showing thin white strata through the red, fossils from the Far North that resulted in the identification of at least sixteen new species of extinct marine organisms, and always the temperature and general weather conditions.[14] Because he was the first scientist to venture into areas of northern America, every piece of information Kennicott supplied added immeasurably to the scarce data. Now, on the Western Union expedition, Kennicott and his scientists would have the same heady opportunity to be the first to record new and surprising information.

When they reached the eastern isthmus port of Greytown, Nicaragua, they learned that very low water in the river would make their transit to the west much more difficult than expected. For six days they lay at anchor a quarter mile from land because the now-impassible sand bar blocked all harbor traffic. The naturalists made use of the time and inconvenience by collecting what specimens they could to send back to Washington. Kennicott acknowledged being ill a few days at Greytown, "from the most unpardonable imprudence," he wrote Baird.[15]

When they finally started to cross the isthmus, so many things went wrong that Dall suggested they "hire a man to do the swearing; the entire party can't do the subject justice."[16] Even a routine transit required passengers to change ships several times. On this transit one of the ships sprang a leak and slowly settled into the mud, forcing the passengers to wait to be rescued by a sister ship. At another point, the low water prevented all ships from operating. To keep everyone moving, Kennicott, Rothrock, and Dall, up to their waists in water, physically hauled rafts full of passengers through portions of the river for two days. It added up to an exhausting crossing of more than two weeks instead of the usual transit of three days. For their trouble, Kennicott was given a sack of gold pieces by the transit company which he immediately shared with those passengers who had also helped.

By the time they reached the Pacific side of the isthmus and transferred to a California-bound steamer, many of the Corps, including Rothrock, Dall, and Kennicott, were ill with fever and with various stomach complaints. The cause may have been conditions on the ship since, as Dall remarked, "The water we use to drink is condensed by the steamer and to use K's words, 'looks just like anyone else's'—from the iron of the condenser, I think."[17] Yet Dall also notes that they "were well bitten by mosquitoes" and names their fever both "Chagres" for that river's drainage area and "Panama" for the general tropical area. Rothrock's fever and headache were treated with ten grains of calomel and ten of jalap, both powerful laxatives thought to expel illness. In anticipation of the same illness, Dall took two grains of Blue Mass as a preventative and wrote his mother "I've taken fearfully of calomel jalap, quinine, and mercury and am now well... I have lost thirty-four pounds, but feel about as usual and am working as usual. For five days, with a constant diarrhea, I didn't eat a particle. About a third of the passengers were sick."[18]

As an introduction to the rigors of exploration and as a hint of the kinds of things that could go wrong, the isthmus crossing gave the men many reasons to change their minds and withdraw from the expedition. No one did.

Since they had been out of communication with the United States for almost three weeks, they had heard nothing about the war. Not only did they not know the result of battles being fought as they left, they had no inkling of Lee's surrender on April 9, 1865, and could not imagine the terrible events of April 14. On April 23, a passing steamer on its way to Mexico changed its course so the captain could shout to them the awful news of President Lincoln's assassination. Combined with the news of the capture of Richmond and the end of the war, the passengers were "an excited crowd and it would not have been safe for anyone to have uttered any secession sentiments...."[19]

Strychnine
2003

Even though Kennicott in Greytown admitted to an "unpardonable imprudence" that might have suggested drinking too much alcohol, my interchange with Dr. Gretchen Worden surprised me.

"A strychnine user?" she asked. "Was he a homeopath?"

"Oh. Umm. I don't know," I wavered. "Why?"

"Strychnine is very good for hangovers. We homeopaths use it all the time."

I'd been referred to Dr. Worden at Philadelphia's Mutter Museum of the College of Physicians because I wanted to talk to an expert about what I thought of as a deadly poisonous chemical. Now, she opened a whole new avenue of investigation: the medical uses of strychnine.

Kennicott had very little strychnine in his remains: 0.0013 micrograms per gram in the abdominal area. Ordinarily, that amount could be easily explained because Kennicott would have followed the Smithsonian's advice to use strychnine in preserving mammal specimens. But, the 0.00336 micrograms per gram in his brain was within the range of the 0.0005 to 0.026 micrograms per gram that can be a fatal dose. Still, fatal doses vary among individuals and there is some suggestion that a tolerance to the

chemical can be acquired.

The basic problem with the strychnine was that, on the expedition, Kennicott had a vial of the small, grayish-brown, translucent crystals at hand and, because of that, his men thought he'd committed suicide by swallowing some. But no one, then or now, wanted Kennicott to be so focused on suicide that he carried the means with him. Could Kennicott have been taking strychnine as a prescribed medication? For what condition? Would Kennicott even have known about homeopathy?

Interestingly, Chicago in the 1800s was one of the centers for homeopathic training. Many doctors, not wanting to cause patients the additional pain of such then-common practices as blistering and bleeding, adopted the approaches of Samuel Hahnemann, a German doctor. His system of homeopathy, introduced in 1796 in Europe, came to the United States around 1825 and reached its popularity peak in the late 1800s. At the time, an estimated one in four doctors recommended, to some degree, homeopathic remedies.[1]

Hahnemann recommended strychnine for a wide variety of conditions, including cases of "stupefaction of the brain... intoxication...vertigo [dizziness]...including the vertigo of syncope [insufficient blood to the brain]."[2] Dosage ranged from 1/60 to 1/10 of a grain. (15 grains equals 1 gram) Because strychnine is a systemwide stimulant, it would have been used in homeopathy to reduce overstimulation. According to Hahnemann, strychnine is "more frequently required by persons who are of an anxious, zealous, fiery, hot temperament ..."[3]

More and more, Kennicott met the description of a homeopathic strychnine patient although he did not seem to recognize his periods of expansive behavior and excessive energy as a problem. Others may have. His uncle wrote to his father when Robert was nineteen: "from what I see of him [Robert] I would caution you to have an eye to him. Try and keep him quiet and calm. He gets unreasonably excited about trifles....He needs no incitement to *do*."[4]

At twenty-five, Kennicott himself reported one period of high energy and overstimulation during his three-year Canadian trip: "From the last of May til June 24...I have been at work generally about eighteen hours out of every twenty-four...we pay little attention to the time of day, but just work as long as we can keep awake.... I was at one time out three days, in which time I slept only once, and then scarce six hours, when I had already been forty-eight hours without sleep. I am making up for last winter's hibernation."[5] He seems to have been very pleased with his energy level. When Kennicott returned from his trip through Canada, his father wrote to Baird, "Bob is back. He is looking well,

but wild to 'fight Indians' in the Secesh.... Bob will write you tomorrow. He is too wild now."[6]

While homeopaths had many wide-ranging uses for strychnine, traditional physicians had just as many. Doctors could find the recommended strychnine doses, along with many other medicines derived from plants, in the medical pharmacopeias of the eighteenth and nineteenth centuries. The sixth edition of Potter's *Compendium* noted, "Nux vomica and its chief alkaloid [strychnine] hold high rank as respiratory, cardiac, muscular and nervous stimulants and stomachic tonics. These powerful poisons are equally powerful remedies for problems such as atonic dyspepsia, gastric catarrh especially of drunkards, constipation, and vomiting [all of them stomach complaints], as well as for tetanus, local paralysis, cardiac failure, and chronic alcoholism."[7] Dr. Harvey Felter, in his *Dispensatory,* stated, "strychnine is more generally employed in troubles affecting the nervous system, bladder, heart, and reproductive organs..."[8] As a stimulant, strychnine made the senses of touch, smell, hearing and vision more acute. In addition, it raised blood pressure.[9] Such an "upper" might be just what a driven explorer like Kennicott needed to keep going on really tough trails in both British and Russian America.

Kennicott's father, Ol' Doc, had a reputation as an herbalist. Might he have prescribed the powerful stimulant? Kennicott seems to have had a personal supply of strychnine on his Canadian exploration sent to him by his family.

Assuming the strychnine he had in the Yukon was also a personal supply, Kennicott may have been taking it – regularly or as needed – for at least seven years.

But how did he know how much strychnine to take? How did he avoid a fatal overdose?

A small pamphlet accompanying a chest of herbals for household use gave the recommended dose for strychnine as the amount that fits on the tip of a pen knife. That short sentence not only indicated how routinely strychnine was used but it also recommended a very common dispenser, a knife everyone could be expected to own. It would not have been unusual for Kennicott to routinely carry such a knife and to use it for many purposes. Because strychnine is a crystal like sugar or salt, only a small amount will stay on the tip of a small knife. As long as Kennicott could stand the very bitter taste of strychnine on his tongue, he could take his dose quickly and without fear of overdosing.

Yet, whether Kennicott used strychnine in homeopathic amounts or in standard prescribed amounts, his low-dose use of strychnine did not cause his death. The half-life of strychnine in humans is ten hours; "chronic poisoning from strychnine is not known and significant cumulative toxicity is not recognized."[10]

There were many good medical reasons for Kennicott to have a personal supply of strychnine. If he had the strychnine since leaving New York, there's no record of his using it in the month it took to reach San Francisco.

San Francisco
Spring 1865

The Scientific Corpsmen were well, if thinner, when they reached San Francisco on April 25, 1865. They found the city's public buildings and private homes draped in black, the flags at half-staff, and the people wearing black crepe arm bands, all in deep mourning over the death of President Lincoln. Nevertheless, Western Union's plans to build telegraph lines simultaneously on two continents separated by an ocean went on. Docks overflowed with the supplies, food, and equipment that the huge and still growing support network required in order to mount two independent expeditions. For example, 79,646 brackets and 80,666 insulators were sent to Plover Bay, Siberia, along with 65 bags of beans, 10 bales of blankets, 25 cases of boots and shoes, 25 cases of bread, 75 bags of potatoes, 25 bales of hops, 76 kegs of sugar, and 10 cases of firearms, among other necessary supplies.

Western Union raised more than $10 million for the enterprise that would string wire over what some calculated to be 5,400 miles: 600 miles in British America, 1,900 miles in Russian America, 400 miles under the Bering Strait, and 2,500 miles in Siberian Russia.[1] Those numbers might have been miscalculations. "From Babine Lake in the centre of British Columbia to the Yukon River in the British Possessions, the country has never been explored, and through this wild region it is the intention of the company to make their way a distance of about 3,000 miles."[2] Which was it: a relatively easy 600 miles in British America or an additional 2,400 unexplored miles?

Information on Russian America was equally speculative. On most maps, even in the highly regarded Johnson's atlas, "the River Youkon is laid down as emptying into the Arctic Ocean near Point Beechy, under the name of River Colville."[3] The whole inland area was so little known that not only was the course of Russian America's large river uncertain, even its spelling had not been codified. Youkon seemed preferred, but Youcan, Yukan, Yudan, Yerkin, and

Yadkin were also in print. The lower reaches of the river had been expertly mapped twenty-five years earlier by the Russian explorer, Lavrenty Zagoskin, but the information was not easily available to the Western world. Even if it had been, the river Zagoskin mapped was named by the Russians the Kwichpak, also with variant spellings. Reasonably informed men debated whether there were two large rivers, the Kwichpak and the Yukon, or one. Kennicott was firmly convinced from his time at Fort Yukon that the Kwichpak and the Yukon were the same river, and that it flowed west from Fort Yukon to the Bering Sea, not north to the Arctic. If he was right, his recommendation to go up the river using a steamboat was the quickest and easiest way to get to Fort Yukon. If he was wrong, as many in the expedition thought, the whole expedition might be imperiled.

Instead of considering this planned sub-Arctic route formidable, if not impossible, Western Union executives heard its advantages: "The land lines firmly planted in the frozen earth will stand as if mortised in rock; no timber to fall across nor sleets to weight the wire, they will stretch over the frozen desolation unharmed and unmolested; besides with reindeer and dogs the winter watching will be comparatively easy."[4] Kennicott warned that slowly moving glaciers could eventually destroy the line and that icebergs in the Bering Strait might cut the line, but neither thought was of enough concern to change the route.

Public approval of the plans and the route was widespread: "It is the intention of the explorers to carry on their inland explorations in the winter time, at which season travel is much better and can be easily performed with snow shoes or with sledges drawn by dogs, the customary mode of traveling in that country. During the winter months, also, the lakes which abound in that country are frozen over, and the progress of travelers is not impeded by swollen streams and broad lakes as is the case during the summer months."[5]

Kennicott knew better, based on his experiences in the Far North. Of course winter travel was possible; he had done it. Yet, even with the best dogs and the warmest native clothing, it was still very strenuous. He wrote Baird, when first discussing the expedition with Western Union, "I see they want me to explore the [inland northern] region from [Fort] Pelly Banks to Stuart's Lake in winter or fall ... that is an affair of more magnitude, danger, and difficulty. I should think twice before I undertook it for any ordinary compensation."[6] The locations he named are hundreds of miles south of the Yukon River.

Kennicott, July 1865, in Western Union uniform. On his cap, his Scientific Corps insignia included a canoe with WU underneath. Above, bolts of electricity pierce a star and emerge behind the canoe.

Now, in San Francisco, the men of the Scientific Corps at last met the man who would make the final plans for the whole expedition, Colonel Charles S. Bulkley, who titled himself their commanding officer. The scientists may not have thought of the expedition as a military exercise, but Bulkley, recently in charge of Union Army telegraph operations, certainly did. Not only was he comfortable with a military organization, he felt that men away in the field would be more orderly under a chain-of-command system. He also believed that the Russian commanders of the forts they were to use would more easily accept and understand an expedition that had a military appearance. As a result, Bulkley gave military titles to the men. Kennicott and other leaders were majors; the Scientific Corps members were lieutenants; workers were privates. Scientific Corps members received $13 a month, a sum that in Rothrock's view accurately reflected the low opinion Western Union had of them.

If any in the Corps objected to the militaristic organization, they adapted quickly. They dutifully showed up at Geimann's military outfitter shop to buy, at their own expense, their uniforms of dark blue wool patterned after those worn in the recent war. In anticipation of being out of the country for many months, Dall went to a dentist for several fillings and a painful extraction. While their personal preparations went well, plans for the American side of the expedition had already derailed.

A year earlier, when outlining his part of the expedition in New York, Kennicott proposed, and the directors accepted, a plan for starting explorations at the mouth of the Yukon River in Norton

Sound on June 1, 1865, and completing the line at the head of the Fraser River in British America by the end of October 1866. Initially, the Western Union men would stay with men of the Russian American Fur Company at their long-established fort on St. Michael's island just off the coast. Then, the workers would move on to other, smaller, Russian coastal forts to build the telegraph line. The starting date Kennicott chose reflected his scientific interest: he needed to be in the Far North for "egging season" to collect the crucial eggs and young of birds. Kennicott also knew his responsibilities to Western Union would be accomplished more easily in spring and summer. But his plans were already jeopardized by their lengthy isthmus crossing; the northern spring was slipping away.

A year earlier, when Kennicott talked with the Western Union Board of Directors, he was treated as a highly regarded consultant who possessed important information essential to their business plan. At that time, Kennicott was offered a position as second in command of the expedition but he declined it believing that Bulkley should be allowed to make his own appointments when he could appraise the men in person. Kennicott's position within the expedition was open to confirmation. Now, in San Francisco, his role had changed in ways he seemed not to recognize. Now, he was but one of many leaders in a very large operation, all of whom required Bulkley's attention and several of whom had equally critical roles in the two-continent expedition. Kennicott's scientific goals were not as highly regarded in San Francisco as they had been in New York.

When Kennicott learned from Bulkley that the Western Union Company had not yet provided a seaworthy, oceangoing ship to transport men and equipment to Russian America, he was furious and impetuously tried to fix the problem. Kennicott boldly drafted telegrams to those Western Union directors he thought of as personal friends: "On my arrival here I find unexpected and needless delays...through the fault of the Directors..."[7] and "For god's sake give him [Bulkley] whatever power he lacks to buy whatever steamer he chooses."[8] While Kennicott's words sounded fiery, he was not alone in his complaints. In the view of another expedition member, the directors in the East dictated "inexpedient plans," caused "most vexatious hindrances," and generally tied the hands of the men whose competence they had hired.[9] At the same time, Kennicott telegraphed Smithsonian Secretary Henry, asking him to request that Captain Charles Scammon, a whaler with valuable experience in northern waters and brother of one of the Chicago Academy directors, be released from military duty to command an expedition ship. Scammon joined almost immediately.

Lacking a ship to achieve Kennicott's original plan, and rather than waste time, Bulkley decided to begin explorations for the Yukon telegraph line from the southern end of the route. He instructed Kennicott to draft new plans starting from Vancouver/New Westminster, British Columbia and using an inland route north via the Fraser River. Kennicott's new plans reveal not only his optimism and energy but also how little was known about the area that Western Union wanted to use for its line. Kennicott proposed an itinerary that was very specific when it began at Vancouver/New Westminster: "Leave New Westminster May 18, arrive at Ft. Yale (by steam) May 18; above Fort Alexander (by turnpike) May 28; ...to [Fort] St. James (water) June 8."[10] His information on the area north of Fort St. James, inland from the Queen Charlotte Islands, was less specific. He expected to reach Babine Lake on June 12, and be at Dease Lake by July 1, a distance of 300 or 350 miles, he guessed with a question mark. Then, he planned to be at the mouth of the Yukon by July 30.[11] Maps of the time show little detail of the inland area north of the Queen Charlotte Islands. On today's maps, the straight-line distance from Dease Lake to the mouth of the Yukon is twice as far as the distance between Vancouver and Dease Lake. Even though his was a plan for the auspicious summer time, Kennicott allowed an optimistic six weeks to cover the known territory, but just a scant four weeks to cover the unknown.

Kennicott also made other preparations. Three days after they arrived, (April 27) he split his responsibilities, giving management to Dall as the Scientific Director of Natural History operations but keeping for himself Chief of Explorations. He added the twenty-five-year-old telegraph expert Franklin L. Pope to the group as a practical engineer and appointed Rothrock as his Chief of Staff, even though Dall observed "just now he [Rothrock] seems to want the confidence in K. that the position should demand."[12] Kennicott also hustled about San Francisco, checking the availability of supplies, noting their prices, and filling out requisitions in the slapdash, non-military style he liked best but that irritated Bulkley. Even though Dall observed that Kennicott "has very little method in his work,"[13] Kennicott himself bragged about the amount of

Dall, July 1865, in full Western Union uniform. His insignia featured a bug on his cap and scallop shells on his shoulders.

work he accomplished: "In short, did six weeks work in less than ten days."[14]

Kennicott's hyperactivity and constant reporting of his actions to Bulkley did not impress his commander. By May 7, just two weeks after arriving, Dall recognized "some misunderstanding between him [Kennicott] and Bulkley owing probably to K's rapid and somewhat incoherent style of talking and perhaps also partly to K's somewhat overambitious views with regard to his position in the Expedition. In the evening K takes Rothrock and I up to Bulkley's room where he broaches his plan of going by Stickeen [river] and Dease Lake with fifty men and ten thousand pounds [of food and equipment], which Bulkley does not receive favorably."[15]

On May 8, "Rothrock is ordered to report to Major Pope and with him to get up a plan of exploring the Babine Lake district. In the evening ... K comes into the discussion in a somewhat excited manner and knocks the whole thing into 'pi.' "[16] The next morning, Dall walked with Kennicott to "try & post him on events somewhat, and give him some idea of how I an outsider view the situation....K writes out a plan for the Youkon, which is fairly received by B[ulkley] & K is instructed to proceed on a basis of ten men and make out specifications. Now at least we are on firmer ground."[17]

But Kennicott was not. Bulkley not only stopped confiding in him or taking his suggestions but also told Kennicott that he "was a green fellow who talked very fast" and who Bulkley "feared had no great executive capacity."[18] As a result, Bulkley suggested Kennicott take some time off. Kennicott visited friends, did some collecting, and took what he called "a good long sleep."[19] In Kennicott's absence, Bulkley ordered Pope to gather twelve men and supplies to go inland up the Fraser River toward the Yukon. Kennicott's handpicked scientists, Rothrock, Elliott, and Bannister, were included in the group, as was the artist Maynard. On his return to Western Union offices, Kennicott was not just angry at being so disgraced but also stunned by what he viewed as the defections of his men. They had been carefully chosen to make new-to-science collections in the Far North; now some were going into previously explored territory where he had already collected hundreds of specimens. He tried to talk the scientists out of leaving, but "the boys…had pretty much made up their minds that the whole Telegraph Expedition was a myth. I could not, of course, tell them what I knew of the real circumstances, but could only bid them wait patiently."[20]

As Kennicott saw it, "they had taken advantage of my supposed disgrace at headquarters to pick the best of the men I had chosen, and who were pledged to go with them ere I could know it. To get Henry Elliott (whom I needed for Nat. Hist. Purposes) flattered into a state of mind where I could not control him — and that they, while using my ideas, my knowledge, the very requisitions I had made out, made a great show of refusing all advice or assistance from me."[21]

Dall could understand their refusal: "Write for Mr. Kennicott being with him all day [May 10]. He is certainly in a great state of excitement or else he was intoxicated. I should say of another man judging from the same data that he was either insane or incapable of doing the work set before him. It is now since last October he has been running a full head of steam of excitement and whiskey. He is absurdly suspicious of everyone."[22] Writing his memoirs sixty years later, Dall's view of the events had mellowed: "Kennicott's enthusiastic manner and boyish traits were brought up against him and violent antagonism to him and his advice was exhibited by a clique…. The opposition rose to such a pitch that some members of our little scientific party became afraid of its dissolution…and seized the chance of joining a party which proceeded to British Columbia…."[23]

Four members of the Scientific Corps left with the Fraser River group on May 17, 1865, taking along letters of introduction that Kennicott wrote to those friends in the Hudson's Bay Company who were most likely to meet Pope's party as they went through British Columbia. Kennicott, "nearly worn out with anxiety and excitement," joined in the hearty good cheer at the dock when the party boarded the steamer *Sierra Nevada* for British Columbia. He returned to his hotel room, and "while sitting on the edge of the bed, talking to one of his companions, the color suddenly left his cheek, and he fell back pulseless for several minutes on the bed. The immediate production and use of the strongest brandy by his friend brought him through this attack…."[24]

Kennicott seemingly paid little attention to this "faint," just as he ignored the "vertigo" in Chicago four months earlier, and was out of his hotel room the next morning when Dall called on him. While Kennicott often wrote freely of his regularly recurring, low-energy states, calling them "torpor," "semi-comatose," and "lethargy," he did not write of his near-death experience to anyone. Nor did he, at the time, write anyone that his handpicked scientists had left him to go with another leader. Instead, on May 22, Kennicott sent a circumspect and blandly factual wire to Baird: "Rothrock, Bannister, Elliott, and Maynard have gone up Fraser River en route to Flag Lake and the Youkon. Charles Pease goes with me [to Norton Sound], and Dall with Bulkley [around the ports of call]. Bischoff not yet placed...."[25] Kennicott made the upsetting event that split his Scientific Corps sound like a planned dispersal of his men but wrote philosophically later, "Boys are rather failures when one attempts to do men's work with them."[26] Still, in an even later letter, he accepts some of the responsibility: "Had I only been an old...sober-looking slow coach, less communicative and energetic, I believe I should have been allowed to put this thing through."[27]

California and Montgomery Streets, San Francisco, 1865.

The Pulseless Faint 2006

Having read the account of Kennicott's pulseless faint in the *Transactions of the Chicago Academy*, I wanted to see the account of it in Dall's diary since he was the only one who recorded what happened in San Francisco.

But there was no diary entry describing the faint. Was it possible the man who noted Kennicott's episode of vertigo in Chicago simply didn't note a complete faint in San Francisco only four months later? Not likely. Uncharacteristic.

Could it be that Dall wasn't in the room when it happened?

But Dall said he was with Kennicott. He wrote Mary Kennicott on September 27, 1866, when he learned her son was dead: "I was with Robert last year in San Francisco when he had an awful attack of the same palpitation, brought on by anxiety and care. I was by him, nursed him tenderly and he pulled through bravely."[1]

That last sentence can't be accurate. Nor is the last phrase of the *Transactions* account, "...he was confined to his room for several days." Dall's own diary contradicts those words. Dall says he "went to call on Kennicott" the morning after the fainting event but Kennicott wasn't in the hotel. Three days later, Kennicott went to the opera. As for tenderly nursing him, the only mention of anything like that

was days earlier when Dall bought laudanum for Kennicott's diarrhea.

So, what does that letter to Mary Kennicott really say? Yes, Dall was "with Robert in San Francisco" — so were the rest of the Scientific Corps. But the letter doesn't say "with him when he fainted." Then what "attack" could Dall be talking about? Not, it seems, an attack like a fainting episode when the heart stops beating, but a "palpitation brought on by anxiety and care." Palpitation means "beating rapidly and strongly." Could Dall be describing Kennicott's many weeks of high-energy, excitable behavior in San Francisco and not the single event of his fainting? Was Dall suggesting that Kennicott had a pattern of medical events, palpitations, that led to his death? Or, was Dall just trying to comfort a grieving mother by suggesting that her son had been doing his best and that Dall had tried to help?

What does the *Transaction* paragraph really say? At the time of the faint, Kennicott was talking to "one of his companions." The life-saving brandy was given "by his friend." Why was the account so vague? Who was there to save Kennicott?

Kennicott and Pease stayed at the Cosmopolitan Hotel; Dall stayed at the American Exchange Hotel. When Dall "called on" Kennicott the following morning, he walked from one hotel to the other, not just down the hall. If he had been in the room when Kennicott fainted, and if the event was as serious as he wrote to Mrs. Kennicott, he would have known where Kennicott was, in bed, and wouldn't have "called." Most probably, Dall wasn't there.

Then, who was? If the companion was a member of the expedition, Pease was the most likely person. Not only did they have rooms in the same hotel, but Pease was a longtime friend to whom Kennicott could speak openly. After all, what would Kennicott want to talk about immediately after his scientists had left him, and he had been demoted, and others had suggested he was incompetent? Also, there was brandy at hand. Who would Kennicott drink with after an upsetting day?

Assuming Pease was Kennicott's life-saving companion, the fainting event may not have been known to anyone else at the time. Nothing would be gained by mentioning it. Dall's diary entries show he certainly didn't know. Besides, Kennicott was out and about the next day as if nothing had happened. In fact, he probably was fine; it was a transitory, if frightening, event.

View from the Cosmopolitan Hotel, 1865

San Francisco
Summer 1865

Three weeks later, perhaps in reaction to his pulseless faint, Kennicott began an account sent to Baird, "Should anything happen to me on this Expedition so that I never return...."[1] Kennicott wanted to dispute any charge that he had not done the work asked of him or had not prepared properly for the expedition. He defended his May actions through a forty-page document, disjointed, difficult to follow, and written in various hands. He revealed, "Except Charlie Pease, most of my 6 men from the East hurt me by their childish impatience and distrust in me. I'm afraid Rothrock even was not quite as trustful in me as he might have been and so hurt me by encouraging the idea that I was not competent to perform the work. Bannister also strange to say backed out of his allegiance to me."[2]

Yet, Kennicott was not dismissed from the expedition. Instead, as the Fraser River group left, Bulkley asked him to revive his initial plans for going into Russian America using the Yukon River from its delta. Essentially, Bulkley tried to make the best of the irritating, shipless delay by splitting his American continent men into two groups that would attack the installation of the telegraph line from each end and meet in the middle. In typically upbeat fashion, Kennicott made the most of the new arrangements and wrote very positively about the expedition's Scientific Department that Bulkley established with him at its head. Kennicott seemed genuinely pleased to be ordered to make as thorough an exploration of natural history as possible, a goal of his from the beginning, and to have the responsibility of fewer men.

In the new version of his plans to explore the Yukon River from its mouth to Fort Yukon, Kennicott assumed the party would land at the Russian Fort St. Michael's in Norton Sound on June 1 and would use a steamboat to ascend the river.[3] Even though much of the river remained uncharted, using it was the better plan; even less was known about the surrounding land. By using the steamer against the oceanbound current of the Yukon, Kennicott predicted it would take a month from landing on the coast to be at the Great Bend of the Yukon, just above the Russian Fort Nulato, and then another two weeks to be at the British Fort Yukon.

To Kennicott's complete frustration, the Yukon group did not reach St. Michael's on June 1, 1865. Instead, they spent that day in San Francisco, joining other citizens in a National Fast Day called by President Johnson, an opportunity for the whole nation, as distinct from groups or individuals, to lament the assassination of Lincoln and to pray for guidance.[4] Knowing what the extensive delay meant, Kennicott wrote Baird on June 4, "I considered I could not with honor back out—and had calmly made up my mind to forgo any extensive Natural History operations for this year...."[5] With that, Kennicott abandoned his primary reason for joining the Western Union Telegraph Expedition.

Then, the Yukon group spent the whole month of June, plus two weeks of July, in San Francisco. Kennicott needed to shop for proper clothes; everything he had packed had been lost or stolen during the awful isthmus crossing. With nothing much else to do, Kennicott, Dall, Pease, and Bischoff became tourists. They explored San Francisco, which Dall described as a poor city, its buildings "especially mean, no fine one except it be a hotel." Even twenty years after the gold rush, San Francisco still seemed a boom town, not a sophisticated city. Dall marveled, though, at the celebrated Washington Market: "Never saw any market surpassing it. Vegetables and fish especially remarkable."[6] Kennicott called San Francisco a sink of iniquity, a view Dall confirmed by observing "..the Company uniform adorned the brothel, the streets, and not infrequently, the ditch.... All the bummers and rumsuckers imaginable were 'on the Expedition.' "[7]

Kennicott interviewed some of the hundreds of men who applied to join the telegraph expedition but whose prospects were limited because many of the men needed to install and wire the telegraph poles had been hired in the East. Kennicott's small group of explorers, limited to ten men including his scientists, was filled, until a very persuasive local, George Adams, described the coming hardships in the north to two men who then quit. In their place, Adams convinced Kennicott to hire him and his friend Frederick Smith. Adams was determined to be part of the telegraph expedition because, as a boy of thirteen, he "took an enthusiastic part in the procession" in San Francisco celebrating the transatlantic telegraph, for him the "outstanding event of the age."[8]

His view was shared by many as, on September 1, 1858, the whole nation officially celebrated the first successful sending and receiving of messages between Europe and America. A telegraph cable resting on the floor of the Atlantic Ocean between Valentia Island, Ireland, and Trinity Bay, Newfoundland, that took three attempts to lay, finally let Queen Victoria and President Buchanan congratulate each other on August 16, 1858.

George Adams in WU uniform showing the snowshoe worn on the shoulder straps of Scientific Corpsmen.

New York City celebrated the accomplishment for forty-eight hours, almost nonstop. Church bells pealed, one hundred guns saluted, thousands of marchers jammed four miles of parade route up Broadway. A day of banquets and speeches was followed in the evening by a firemen's torchlight parade that lit the city like day. The finale, held on the second evening in front of City Hall, featured huge banners with the names of fourteen men who made the cable possible: investors, directors, an electrician, an engineer, and even the man who took the ocean soundings. As the excited crowd watched, two cardboard cable-laying ships moved slowly across the plaza toward each other. A large sign proclaimed, "The electric flash shall belt the earth." When the ships met, a blaze of fireworks filled the sky with colored stars, golden rain, and fiery meteors, ending the celebrating. Similar celebrations, if not as lavish, were held in cities large and small throughout the States. Seven years after those memorable parades, George Adams joined the Western Union Telegraph Expedition hoping to be as celebrated as that, especially since the transatlantic cable failed just months after the festivities.

When all the men going to the Yukon were in place, Kennicott helped ensure success by spending, in Dall's calculations, "at least two-thirds of his year's salary during the last few weeks of our stay in Frisco in lending these men money, treating them like brothers and endeavoring to create a clannish feeling among them that would carry them through difficulty and danger which they will meet."[9] In an earlier attempt to forge a team spirit as well as to comply with Bulkley's military style, Kennicott designed insignia for his Scientific Corps. He decided that his group would be called "Carcajous" and would wear a small silver snowshoe on their shoulder straps, a miniature gold canoe on their caps. All of these recalled for Kennicott his three-year trip through British America when he first experienced snowshoes, Hudson's Bay Company canoes, and the French traders' name for the clever, tenacious wolverine. That these insignia had little meaning to the others in the Scientific Corps is made clear by Dall's diary entry on the day the defecting scientists left for British Columbia: "Cheer them, well away, *Caribous*, and return."[10]

When Kennicott appointed Dall as head of natural history to keep Western Union's attention focused on scientific matters, Dall designed his own insignia. At the end of June 1865, he showed them to Kennicott and had them made quickly before they sailed for the Yukon. Giving his title inaccurately, he wrote his father he would wear "as Director of the SCT [Scientific Corps telegraph] operations shoulder straps with two silver scallop shells on each and a little gold bug in my cap."[11] He also had the tailor add gold braid to his uniform trousers.

To help while away the idle days in San Francisco, Kennicott had a letter of introduction to the scientific community from Smithsonian Secretary Henry. Dall had letters of introduction from Reverend Robert Collyer of Chicago, from the Kennicotts, and from his relatives in Baltimore. In Victorian America, everyone needed to be formally and properly introduced, otherwise the doors of private homes were often closed to newcomers. Kennicott and Dall were received graciously by many of the prominent members of San Francisco society. It is possible that the scientists found more doors open to them in San Francisco than they did in Washington because the social conventions were different.

In the East, it was not always socially acceptable to be known as a scientist, particularly one who studied the natural world after Darwin suggested the theory of evolution, because science seemed to pit its knowledge against the belief of religion. "In those days," Dall later commented, "a young student of science was a doubtful character in the minds of many good people, was suspected of designs on religion unless he attended church regularly, [and also] of unknown but dreadful tendencies to dissipation."[12] The rumors of dissipation circulated because the alcohol scientists used to preserve specimens could be rum, brandy, whiskey, or wine as well as ethanol and isopropanol.

In the West, peopled by secular businessmen, Buddhist Chinese, Orthodox Russians, and others, Kennicott's non-attendance at church may not have been as important. That same polyglot of successful people, speaking English with different accents, also may have blurred the social distinctions Easterners placed on Kennicott's broad Midwestern accent and Dall's Boston Brahmin accent. Then, too, being part of an economic engine as forceful as the Western Union Telegraph Expedition may have offered a place at many local tables.

One of the homes open to Kennicott was that of the Russian consul, Martin Klinkofstrom. The consul, his wife, and two young-Miss daughters may have genuinely appreciated the ebullient, high-energy scientist who was witty, sociable and told captivating stories of his explorations. Or, the consul may simply have been conducting subtle diplomacy with a prominent member of a large American enterprise, since Kennicott was the one member of the expedition who had been in Russian America, at British Fort Yukon.

The Russians allowed the British fort to exist because it was at the far eastern edge of their territory; territory the Russians were trying to sell. Ten years earlier, in 1854, Russia suggested the United States buy their territory because they feared Britain would simply annex the land during the Crimean War to complete their possession of the top of the Western world. At the time, the government of the United States was not interested. But by 1860 the concept of Manifest Destiny, under which the US would acquire Mexico, British America and Russian America, was more popular. Now that the Civil War, in which Britain supported the Confederacy, was over, Russia again approached the United States, mentioning that it was also working out a land-lease deal with Britain. William Seward, an ardent expansionist appointed secretary of state in Lincoln's and then Johnson's cabinet, brought the purchase proposal to President Johnson. So, the Russian consul's hosting of Kennicott may have been a way to positively influence the explorer's future reports on the territory for sale.

No matter why he was invited, Kennicott spent many evenings with the consul's family. Dall accompanied Kennicott on the evening of May 20 "to hear [the opera] Norma with K., Captain and Mrs. Scammon, Miss Bowline and the daughter of a Russian gentleman, a very pretty girl Miss Olga Klinkofstrom."[13] Dall evidently enjoyed the evening and the company because he records thirteen other events with the Kinkofstroms, eight of them with Kennicott as well. On July 4, Dall and Kennicott rented a hotel room having a balcony and also provided chairs so that "the ladies

Klink, Mrs. Klink and family, Miss de Ro, Mrs. Scammon" could view the anniversary parade in comfort and safety. Dall was hoping for a celebration such as Boston would have produced. Instead, he found the parade "poor, the military and naval blacks and whites making all the show."[14] Even the fireworks disappointed him. On July 6, Dall and Kennicott had their pictures taken in their uniforms and on July 9 Kennicott joined Dall, who had been to church with the Klinkofstroms, to "get a number of photos including Olga and Charlotte [de Ro]."[15] This practice of exchanging photographs was commonly done before long trips to provide mementos for both the traveler and those at home.

No one knew why the expedition had been delayed so long, but Adams suggested that at least part of the cause was the fourth attempt to lay the transatlantic cable. When, on July 7, Bulkley received word that the attempt failed, he rushed preparations for the Western Union Telegraph Company's Extension of the Collins Overland Telegraph. In a July 25 letter, Bulkley indicts the Navy Department and their "unwilling disposition to favor us."[16] In an official report, Bulkley asserts he was awaiting the arrival of goods from the East.[17] All of those reasons may be true.

July 4 Parade on Second Street, San Francisco, 1865.

Transactions 2007

Could I accept what I read as true if I didn't know who wrote it?

Transactions of the Chicago Academy of Sciences Volume I, Part II uses Kennicott's own letters to give an excellent account of his three-year expedition through British America. But information relating to the two years he spent with the telegraph expedition is condensed into ten pages and contains nothing directly from Kennicott. Instead, the Academy resorted to the next best person, without identifying him by name: "For the following history of the last year of his [Kennicott's] life, and the unexpected difficulties met with in the prosecution of his design, the committee are indebted to a fellow-officer of the expedition, a friend who stuck by him until death, and who did his best to finish the work he had begun."[1]

As one-third of the published sources about Americans in the Yukon (the others are the diaries of Bannister and Adams), the authorship of *Transactions* was very important to deduce. If it had been written by an eyewitness, it would be viewed as an accurate accounting of events. Written by anyone else, its truthfulness could be questioned.

Only four Scientific Corpsmen went with Kennicott to the Yukon: William Dall, Charles Pease, Henry Bannister, and Ferdinand Bischoff. Bischoff wasn't an officer in the expedition and stayed in Sitka the whole year. Bannister did not "stick by" Kennicott but initially joined the Fraser River exploring party. Charles Pease is given credit for the *Transactions* section by James Alton James, author-editor of *The First Scientific Exploration of Russian America and the Purchase of Alaska*. But James does not explain his conclusion, and I couldn't agree. My most obvious objection was that Pease did not "do his best to finish the work;" he left both Nulato and Russian America as soon as he could. Instead, I felt a very strong case could be made that the section in *Transactions* was written by Dall.

True, both Dall and Pease stuck by Kennicott; but there the similarity ends. Dall was a trained scientist who worked with Kennicott at the Chicago Academy and was known to the Academy president. Because of that, Dall was likely to be asked to write for them. There were no references to Pease visiting Chicago or the Academy. Dall was named a commanding officer by Kennicott, in fact, installed as his replacement as head of natural history. Pease wasn't an officer. In addition, Pease gave himself credit for finding Kennicott's body in a letter to his relatives; *Transactions* gives the credit to other people. If Pease were the author of *Transactions*, wouldn't he have continued to give himself the credit? Even more telling, I noticed as I read the various documents that Dall's personal letters were written in the same emotional style as was the Yukon section of *Transactions*. They sound alike.

Confirmation of Dall's authorship turned up in his files in the Smithsonian Archives. In 1926 Dall wrote an unpublished, personal "Memoir to My Grandchildren" in which he states, "Robert Kennicott was a most loveable character, an account of whose life, partly contributed by me, will be found in the *Transactions of the Chicago Academy of Sciences*."[2] Accepting Dall as the author of the section relating to the Western Union expedition means that the information in it is not fully trustworthy. Not only was Dall not a witness to Kennicott's trials in the Yukon and death at Nulato, but he must have relied on information from other people, and must have composed his words fully two years after the events.

Furthermore, Dall wrote about Kennicott for a specific audience: Not only would members of the Academy, in Kennicott's home town, read his account but so would Kennicott's mother, siblings, relatives, and close friends. Dall had every incentive to portray his mentor in the very best possible light.

Unfortunately, knowing who wrote *Transactions* made an important third of the published information about Kennicott and the expedition less reliable.

Unidentified paddle-wheel steamer in Bannister's diary.

To the Yukon
Summer 1865

"A fine vessel and beautifully fitted up," decided Dall when he viewed the bark-rigged *Golden Gate* at the wharf in San Francisco. On board, headed for Russian America's Norton Sound, he was a little less enthusiastic. "The *Gate* skips along as merrily as a young goat and Davis asks me piteously if she isn't going to tip over as she bends under the stiff breeze. Feel some bilious symptoms and take two of my own pills."[1]

At last, the reduced Scientific Corps and the telegraph workers sailed on July 13, 1865, three and a half months after leaving New York and, most critically, almost six weeks after Kennicott had originally expected to be at the mouth of the Yukon River. When they left San Francisco, the steamer *Wright* carried Bulkley; the *Gate* carried Kennicott and the Scientific Corps: Pease, Dall, and Bischoff.

In the idle days on board, Kennicott had time to revise, once more, his plans for the Yukon. He had reassured Baird, "No going home for me 'til I've accomplished something big and the harder it seems the more I won't give up."[2] But, as the summer passed, Kennicott became more concerned about the conditions they would find in the North. Not only were they missing the best of the whole collecting season, but more to the point, they were missing the chance to hunt, fish, and trap their own food for the winter ahead, a potentially life-threatening problem. Kennicott realized, "I am to try what would, I suppose, be called a dangerous expedition considering the season and circumstances....I am

In Bannister's diary.

W.U.T. Coo Barque Golden Gate

Capt. C. M. Scammon U.S.R.S.

Ounga Island (off Alaska)

Sep'r 30th 1865.

(Drawn from memory)

to go up the Youkon — I must make most of the distance in winter. I may have a tough time — but mal de raquette [from walking on snowshoes] will be charming by contrast with the infernal time I've had here..."[3] in San Francisco.

In San Francisco Kennicott, the expert, had many of his informed proposals ignored. One, rejected immediately by Bulkley, called for fifty men and ten thousand pounds of food and equipment to go inland up the temperate climate of the Fraser River. In his next request, for his own men ascending the northern Yukon in a steamer, Kennicott insisted that "10 times the ordinary ration of tea, 3 times the ordinary ration of sugar, [and] nearly double the ordinary ration of other food will be required in this climate."[4] He did not receive them. Kennicott worried, "It is very evident to me that Bulkley does not at all appreciate the true difficulties he will have to contend with in the Youkon region....He expects men to subsist on the Army ration and cook with Army utensils, etc, etc..."[5] However, the "true difficulties" were not going to be Bulkley's to experience, but Kennicott's.

Costs were, of course, important to Western Union. Even the astonishing amount of money dedicated to the telegraph expedition was evidently still not enough to meet everyone's expectations. Kennicott complained, "I have thus far not been allowed to choose my own outfit and have been absolutely obliged to purchase many articles myself which the co. ought to have furnished...."[6] Among them were a sextant and a barometer, basic tools for Kennicott's explorations. A telegraph explorer in Siberia, who also lacked a sextant, additionally complained that he was given useless tent covers instead of the tents he requested. Dall's complaint when the Fraser River group left San Francisco reflected not only the company's economies but also the social structure of the time. The company saved money by buying the educated scientists steerage tickets on the boat where they would be, Dall fumed, "neck and neck with chain gangs of coolies for the mines."[7] Later, as his own Yukon-bound group was leaving San Francisco, Dall complained of more critical things. He had been appointed as ship's doctor but considered the medical supplies so inadequate that he bought some himself, along with the scales to weigh the medicines out. Dall was so fed up that he had "a spat with K. about the parsimony of the company" to the point of "blow[ing] off steam on the subject of the Expedition. D__n it. I have lost all confidence in our commander

[Bulkley] and in the value of this year's operations, not only in scientific but telegraphic purposes."[8] He later concluded in exasperation, "It will be a direct interposition of Divine Providence if this Expedition ever comes to success under existing conditions."[9]

Dall's concern was not for himself. While starting out with Kennicott's party, Dall was not going to land with them but rather continue around the ports of call on the Western Union ship where he would be able to make scientific collections when the ship stopped in the Siberian port of Plover Bay and the Kamchatka Peninsula port of Petropavlovsk. Since the waters of Russian America would be frozen, making Dall's expertise in marine life useless there, Kennicott ordered Dall to return to San Francisco and do what he could to keep Western Union focused on scientific efforts. Dall would collect in the Yukon the next summer.

Kennicott's mother, when informed of these new arrangements, wrote Dall, "[Bob] does not seem to me strong enough to bear the hardships and fatigue that I know he will have to encounter....I am more sorry than I can tell you, that you do not remain with Bob. I felt sure whilst you were with him that you would be a good friend. Now I don't see that anyone I know will be in his party."[10] The Yukon-based Scientific Corps at this point was Kennicott, Bischoff, and Pease.

Even with the delayed start, the ships did not sail directly to Russian America. At a reconnoitering stop in Drake's Bay, Kennicott left his men to join Bulkley's ship. Then, the *Gate* sailed directly to Sitka, Russian America, but the *Wright* steamed to Victoria, British Columbia, first. There Kennicott obtained additional equipment designed specifically for Arctic exploration from his friends at the Hudson's Bay Company.

In Victoria, in July 1865, Kennicott learned that the Confederate ship, *Shenandoah*, had recently sunk whaling ships in the area, a reminder that, despite the Civil War's conclusion in April, the fighting had not stopped. The *Shenandoah*'s captain, James Waddell, refused to accept the truth of Lee's surrender and continued his destruction of whaling ships in order to ruin that large sector of the Union economy. In total, he destroyed thirty-seven vessels, the majority whaling ships, and almost all of them after the war was officially over. The captain of one destroyed ship, Hawes of the *Milo*, reported a conversation with Waddell. Hawes remarked that he "first supposed the *Shenandoah* to be one of the Russian telegraph vessels. Captain Waddell rejoined: 'Yes, I am a telegraph.'"[11] It seemed that, like the telegraph, the *Shenandoah* would continue to send its messages.

Kennicott also learned, to his surprise, that Bannister, who had left in May with the Fraser River party, was now in Victoria and available to go north. Pope and Rothrock sent Bannister back because they thought he would not be able to withstand the rigorous conditions of telegraph work in British Columbia. Kennicott and Bannister may have been embarrassed to see each other. Bannister, after all, deserted the man who had enlisted him and who had convinced his parents he could go on this expedition. Kennicott, in his anger at the defections, somehow blamed Bannister for encouraging the other scientists to leave and even complained to Bannister's father about his actions. Nevertheless, Kennicott now invited Bannister to be part of the Yukon River party.

Also at Victoria, Frederick Whymper, a British artist, signed on to take the place of the artist Maynard who had gone with the Fraser River party. The arrangement was probably made by Baird who was determined to have a visual record of the expedition; Kennicott referred to Whymper as "your artist" in a letter to Baird.[12] Unfortunately, Whymper was only allowed to board the ship; he would not be allowed to land with the scientists. Baird would not have a pictorial record of the first year but Whymper could land next year.

From Victoria, Kennicott wrote Baird several letters. In one, he recognized that it was too late for the summer's hunting and collecting; in another, perhaps related to the information in the first, he reported, "I am sick, disgusted, and almost disheartened. I have a chronic fit of the blues and am getting as sulk as to be absolutely worthless."[13] At the same time, he wrote his brother "When I left San Francisco two weeks since I fell into one of my habitual semi-comatose states and am now as torpid as a tortoise in January.... When I wake from my present torpor, however, and have a chance to begin work I shall regain my energy and courage and will then enjoy the expedition all the more by contrast with my painfully idle life in San Francisco."[14] Dall recalled years later, "The opposition and incredulity with which his sound advice had been met... had depressed his usually exuberant spirits and the desertion of some members of his selected party worried him."[15] With the return of one of the deserters, the Yukon Scientific Corps was now

Kennicott, Bannister, Bischoff, and Pease.

Kennicott and the additional men steamed off to Sitka, capital of Russian America with a population of eight hundred Russians and three thousand natives, where they arrived on August 10 before the *Gate* did. They stayed thirteen days at this rainy "backwoods post" where "licentiousness, gambling, drinking are carried much farther in proportion than in San Francisco even."[16] They packed natural history specimens to send back to the Smithsonian by returning ships, but put Bischoff ashore because he had developed some blisters on his hands, perhaps from the arsenic used to preserve the specimens. He was left at the hospital to recuperate and then to make what collections he could in the Sitka area. When the *Gate* arrived, the small steamship, *Lizzie Horner,* was transferred to her. Bannister and Whymper also shipped onto the *Gate* while Kennicott remained on the *Wright*. The Scientific Corps Kennicott had sacrificed his salary to include in the expedition now consisted of Bannister, a neophyte scientist, and Pease, a sometime scientist.

The twenty-one-gun salute as they left Sitka was the last sound any of the Western Union expedition members would hear from the Western world. The company ships were essentially supply ships for all ports on both continents, making long circular trips from San Francisco. They did not sail back and forth between ports, keeping contact with the men, because these northern ports iced over, making them inaccessible from October through May. Kennicott and his men would be completely out of reach by the West and Western Union until the next summer.

Along the beautiful scenery of the peninsula and islands of the archipelago, the steamer and the sailing ship planned to travel together, with the *Wright* towing the *Gate* some of the time. When the ships stopped to investigate the possibility of mining coal for the *Wright's* boiler, Kennicott and his Corps spent the day collecting and exploring at Coal Harbor, Ounga Sound. "None who saw him [Kennicott] there will forget his high spirits, which were always contagious; and the energy with which he followed his favorite pursuit of animated nature brought a glow to his cheek for the first time since his arrival in San Francisco. Seeing him full of life, fun, and irrepressible energy, it was impossible to resist an impulse of admiration...."[17] Days earlier, from Sitka, Dall wrote Kennicott's mother, "In health, Bob is much better than when he left Frisco. When there he was obliged to stimulate a good deal which ran him down; but he seems to have quite recovered."[18] "To stimulate" was a Victorian phrase meaning "to argue against," a reference to Kennicott's disputes with Bulkley and his own Scientific Corps.

The two ships now sailed further along the Alaskan archipelago, where the warm water of the Pacific Ocean meets the cold of the Bering Sea and often creates huge storms with enormous waves. Within days, the expedition ships became separated. In dense fog on September 1, a cry of "breakers dead ahead" sent all of the men of the *Gate* working the sails to prevent their crashing on unseen rocks. "In fifteen minutes more we should have been on them and probably not a soul of us would have been left to tell the tale," said Smith.[19] Next, on September 9, the *Gate* was "rolling like all possessed"[20] in a violent storm. "The waves ran mountains high. Our main yard arms touching the water at nearly every roll."[21] In one roll, Adams was washed by the sea across the deck, where a cannon, tipped up by the lurch, came down and pinned his arm to the deck, saving him from going overboard. Fortunately, his arm was only badly bruised, not broken. After the storm passed, "We had baffling winds for the next 4 days," Bannister relates, "and were 2 days trying to get through Oonamack Passage" into the Bering Sea.[22]

The two ships, no longer even visible to each other, struggled on by themselves to St. Michael's Island in Norton Sound. Kennicott and Bulkley could not have been sure that anyone on the *Gate* was still alive. In turn, the men on the *Gate* did not know whether their leaders on the *Wright* had survived the storm.

St. Michael's Fall 1865

The *Wright* was not there!

The men strained their eyes when the *Gate* came in sight of St. Michael's Island on September 12, 1865, but the steamer was not there. Everyone feared the worst and wondered how they would manage without their leader. Then, to their cheers, Kennicott rowed out to meet them. The *Wright* had arrived days earlier and, aware of the coming ice of winter, had gone on to its other ports of call.

As eager as the men may have been to get off their ship after two long and recently harrowing months at sea, they still must have been surprised to see that their destination was a low-lying island, covered in long, wide-bladed grass, completely without trees, only a short distance from the mainland. Rounding the north curve of the island, they took in a small fort, its red-roofed buildings painted a bright and cheery yellow. Not the image of a military stronghold, but correctly colored to make the fort very visible through fog and snow.

St. Michael's fort and flat, treeless island covered with long, tangled grasses.

Russian American Company flag, 1866

St. Michael's Island, with a thirty-foot-deep volcanic crater in its center, lies sixty miles north of the Yukon River delta. The Russian American Company fort faced the mainland on the southeast side of a small peninsula that curved back toward the island to form a small, secure bay. St. Michael's was a fur-trading and storing fort of significant economic importance to Russia. While not a large place, only about one hundred twenty feet on each side, the fort was reasonably well equipped and fortunately had some supplies to spare for the twenty-seven Western Union men who landed there.

After Kennicott's relief and elation at seeing the men of the *Gate*, he began to discover what he was lacking in equipment and supplies. Items from the *Wright* had been off-loaded onto St. Michael's earlier and now, along with the majority of his supplies from the *Gate*, needed to be moved into the fort for safe keeping. As chief officer, Kennicott reinforced his rank with the Russians and natives by not helping with unloading or transferring the supplies. Instead, he busied himself getting directions and information about the countryside and the route he wanted to take. Since Kennicott usually labored as hard as his men, this change was unusual enough to cause comment.

When the supplies were unloaded, Kennicott complained bitterly to his men about material that had been centrally ordered with very little consultation. He raged about an outfit "in the main improperly selected, negligently protected and hastily delivered."[1] Many of the items designated for the land expedition had instead been used on the ship; some could not be accounted for at all. Among the foodstuffs unloaded were eight thousand pounds of flour and fifteen hundred pounds of bacon. Five hundred pounds of leaf tobacco and two boxes of chewing tobacco that the men could purchase were also in the supplies. For protection and hunting, the group had "5 Sharpe's carbines with 2 boxes of cartridges, 5 antique, worthless rifled muskets with 1 box cartridges, a few poor shotguns, 180 pounds powder with 100 pounds of shot."[2] Some of the flour and gunpowder, that had to last them for at least a year, tipped into the sound from a badly handled canoe. Kennicott sent a furious letter to Baird: "My outfit and equipment for telegraph work is abominable and absurd…we are sent on a forlorn hope with miserable equipment.…I'm going to succeed fully by God if it is only to put myself in a position to punish those who have been the cause of this absurd outfit which is furnished me.

St. Michael's, 1865 showing a free-standing tower and the steamer, Lizzie Horner.

I'm not <u>afraid</u>, but I do feel a little serious at starting with an outfit in the choice of which I've scarce had any voice."[3]

At the end of a hard day of lifting and moving barrels and boxes, the laboring men discovered some alcohol in the supplies and they helped themselves. Kennicott forcibly disarmed one man who was drunk enough to threaten others with a knife, then he poisoned the alcohol to prevent any further such problems.[4]

Worse was to come. Because Kennicott had argued convincingly that the Kwichpak/Yukon River could be ascended by steamer, he had been provided the small, thirty-five-foot *Lizzie Horner.* She had cost an initial $3 thousand and then had been sheathed and coppered to resist ice as well as strengthened inside. Now he discovered she was missing one of her main pipes, carelessly left on the dock at Sitka. The engineer and blacksmith worked to fashion a substitute pipe of copper, but it could not be properly attached. Although the steamer would run for short distances in the calm sound, she could not operate well enough to attempt running against the forceful current of the great river. Within days of landing, the "toy steamer which had been brought at great expense around The Horn,"[5] sat useless in Norton Sound, putting the whole expedition in peril. Smith described the new situation in few words: "This has altered all of the Major's plans, such a thing as the steamer failing us not being thought of."[6]

Kennicott ruefully changed his plans to a completely overland trek, counting on dogs and sleds to move supplies. He acknowledged such a course would make the prospects of success less likely, "We are in a worse predicament than I like to confess to my party. I seriously fear that the Exped. will be pretty much a failure owing to the want of means of transportation. Dogs are not to be had here in any sufficient numbers and the want of snow does not permit sleds to cross to the Kuikpak 'til after this date....Things don't look at all pleasant and I wish I were here quite alone with a small outfit of my own choosing. I could then 'go in' with a lighter heart than I now do when I have the safety and comfort of others to look after."[7] In recognition of his responsibilities, he also repeated his earlier decision, "I leave natural history to Bannister and Pease til next summer when it is my turn at that. I shall pile into the Telegraph work...til Col. Bulkley comes when I hope he will let me resign my present position and work at natural history. I feel determined to effect something good for science ere I leave here if it can be done."[8]

Kennicott had multiple reasons to want to achieve success in science. The Chicago Academy and the recently burned Smithsonian were counting on exotic animal specimens. His friend Stimpson had helped map the Russian American coast; surely Kennicott would be able to map inland areas just as completely. His mentor Baird had staked his reputation on recommending him to Western Union. Kennicott's reputation as explorer/collector/scientist would suffer if he failed. Success was the only option.

When the *Gate* left St. Michael's on September 17, 1865, it carried away Dall, Whymper, and the letters the Western Union men wrote to friends and family. Dall took personal charge of Kennicott's letters to his mother, Baird, Consul Klinkofstrom, and Miss Olga Klinkofstrom. There probably would not be another chance to send a message to anyone until next summer.

Bulkley, who had left before the *Gate* arrived, confidently reported to the Western Union board: "Mr. Kennicott, dividing his party, will explore the country between the Kvichpak, in latitude 60° North, and the Head of Norton Sound; at the same time push his little steamer up the river, until stopped by the ice, then with dogs and sledges reach Fort Youkon....At St. Michael's we found reliable testimony in regard to Kvichpak and Youkon being the same river, and a large, navigable stream filled with islands...."[9] Kennicott's earlier, insistent views on this last point had been reinforced.

Bulkley left three orders for Kennicott: to explore the Kwichpak

to prove that it was the Yukon and to determine how best to use it, to treat the natives in a way to make them useful to the expedition, and to discover the shortest practical line for the telegraph. The first two were easy. Bulkley had already heard credible reports from natives who had traveled from Fort Yukon to St. Michael's on the great river. As for the second, Kennicott was known as a quick study of Indian languages and had made friends of all the tribes he had met previously; he could count on getting helpful information from these natives. The third one was acknowledged by all to be the central problem.

Inside Fort St. Michael's, showing the buildings and flag pole indicated at the bottom of Bannister's sketch, p. 71.

The telegraph line was planned to cross the water to Siberia at the narrowest acceptable point. To accomplish that, it was not reasonable to use the Yukon River below its Great Bend because that would take the line far away from the narrowest point. The plan had always been to reach the northern banks of Norton Sound through a land route from the point where the river turns south. But, no Westerner, in fact, no non-native, not even the Russians, had explored that land.

Without the steamer, St. Michael's was not in a good position for Kennicott's exploration purposes: it was not near the Yukon itself nor any good way to reach the Yukon. After conferring with the natives and Russians at the fort, Kennicott quickly determined to use the regular winter route of the native traders, the shortest route from Norton Sound to the Yukon. From a smaller fort sixty miles northeast, it would take six or seven days along the Ulukak River and through a swampy area to get to the Yukon where they could then follow the river to the last Russian fort, Nulato. Beyond Nulato, more than four hundred straight-line miles to the east, was the only other fort on the river, the Hudson's Bay Company trading post of Fort Yukon. During the last days of September, with snow already falling, Kennicott moved supplies and equipment north along the coast to Fort Unalacleet on the Ulukak River.

The Western Union men were divided into those who would labor to erect telegraph poles and those who would explore the land to determine the path of the poles. As Chief of Explorations in Russian America, Kennicott initially led nine men: William Ennis, Thomas Denison, Joseph Dyer, Frank Ketchum, Michael Lebarge, Frederick Smith, and George Adams in addition to the Scientific Corps members, Bannister and Pease. Bulkley assigned three more men to Kennicott's group: Oscar Bendeleben, Richard Cotter, and Jay Chappel. Kennicott transferred those three, along with Denison and Dyer, to a group under Ennis, who Kennicott appointed his second in command. Those six men were to explore the area to the north around Norton Sound. To explore the area east along the Yukon, Kennicott kept six as his group: Bannister, Pease, Ketchum, Lebarge, Smith, and Adams. To guide his group, Kennicott hired Simon Evan Lukine, a Russian-native whose family had guided Russians and British for generations and who had been up the river to Fort Yukon.

Kennicott's division of the men was not as equitable as the numbers appear because Bannister and Pease were not to explore but to remain on the coast. Bannister was assigned to the fort at St. Michael's to help keep track of the supplies and to keep detailed meteorological records there, following instructions provided by the Smithsonian. In essence, Kennicott was protecting the men he had encouraged to come on the expedition, his Scientific Corps, from the worst of the explorations to be done in the brutal winter. Dall went back to San Francisco, Bischoff stayed in southern Sitka, Bannister kept records at a coastal fort, and Pease could suit himself.

Bannister's home for the duration, St. Michael's, was a plain stockade fort with walls about ten feet high, garrisoned by about two dozen Russians and additionally protected by six cannon in each of the two blockhouses at opposite corners of the stockade. Inside the stockade were a four-room house for the commander, two warehouses for furs, several residences, separate barracks for married and unmarried workers, a kitchen, and a bathhouse. Outside the stockade were a boat storage shed, fur storehouses, a blacksmith shop, several residences, and a house for native company.[10] A freestanding turret had been built outside the fort as well as a small Eastern Orthodox Church.

Bannister recorded the fort's daily routine. "First we were called to chi [tea], that is, the first morning meal consisting of tea and crackers or bread, at six or seven o'clock. From that time till eleven I employed the time variously, much the same as in any other place. At eleven we were called to the first regular meal, when we had regular courses of soup, meat or fish, and fritters or light pancakes with preserves. After dinner I generally went out hunting or collecting and quite often missed the second chi at 4 pm. At half past seven or eight o'clock we had another meal like the one at eleven only without the soup. The cookery was always excellent and though there was not much variety I never tired of it. I would never ask for better fare. Only the post commander, Stepanoff, dined with us and we had waiters and all the extras."[11] Bannister's room in the fort was painted dark red with a gray line near the ceiling. He probably shared the space with someone else, because it held two beds and two desks. His bed was made up with "a wild reindeer hide with the hair on and with one end sewn into a kind of bag to put the feet in. On top of that…blankets and over all a shawl."[12] In one corner, a large Russian stove could heat the room all day.

The other men, living off the land or at more rustic forts, did not fare as well as Bannister.

An unlabeled fort in Bannister's diary, almost certainly St. Michael's.

Bannister's Code
2003

Bannister wrote in code in the diary he kept at St. Michael's? But I'd read the published diary, in *The First Scientific Exploration of Russian America.* There's no code in the book and no mention of coded sentences.

Nevertheless, said Grove director Swanson, on the original handwritten pages Bannister wrote in something other than English. Swanson had checked: the sentences were not in Russian, not in a Native American tongue. Most intriguing, the longest section in code was written on the day Bannister learned Kennicott was dead.

Did Bannister know why Kennicott died? Did he know of a conspiracy? Was it murder? How could we not work to decipher those words?

Since the diary is held at Northwestern University in their archives, I had a chance to see Deering Library again. It was the main library when I was a graduate student at Northwestern but didn't exist, of course, when Robert Kennicott was the curator of a natural history cabinet at the school, or when Henry Bannister worked for Kennicott there. Yet, because of those connections, Deering Archives holds papers and photos from both Kennicott and Bannister.

Deering Library looks just as I always thought a library should. Tall limestone walls. Gothic towers. In the high-ceilinged reading room, narrow stained glass windows glimmer over long rows of dark wooden tables with lights down their centers. When Northwestern outgrew it, the school built a huge library next door turning Deering into a seriously silent research library still sited in quiet majesty at the head of a long meadow.

To get to the files of carefully kept archives, I followed discreet signs through the busy main areas of the current library, left the bright lights and carpeting for dim lights and cement floors, and wove through underground corridors lined with sepia photographs of events long past. At last, essentially right under the grand, Gothic reading room of Deering, in a medium-sized, file-lined room with tiny windows high above my head, I opened the archival folders. There was very little from Kennicott; even Bannister's files were slim. But there were Bannister's diaries, especially the ones from his year in the Yukon.

The Yukon diaries with their leather covers are very small, almost hand-sized. Each page measures about 6½ inches long and 4 inches wide. Bannister's handwriting is proportionally small. Tiny; squint-provokingly tiny. Some pages are written, some printed in a way that makes them look almost drawn. The pages had faintly ruled lines but were otherwise blank, not divided into days, so Bannister could comfortably write as much or as little as he liked. Fortunately, he used very permanent, dark ink. Equally fortunately, he was precise: there are very few scratch-outs, no blobs of wayward ink. These didn't look like, or read like, spur-of-the-moment impressions and thoughts. What Bannister put down in his diary seemed carefully considered and composed.

And, there was the code.

Only fifteen coded entries on just thirteen different days. Some were only a sentence long. They began in the early spring of 1866 and ended with Bannister's return to the United States later that year. Very odd. They had to be decoded. In Russian America, Bannister was the only diarist who knew Kennicott before the expedition, who

might understand his thinking, who might reveal his basic character.

[To read Bannister's decoded words, see page 124.]

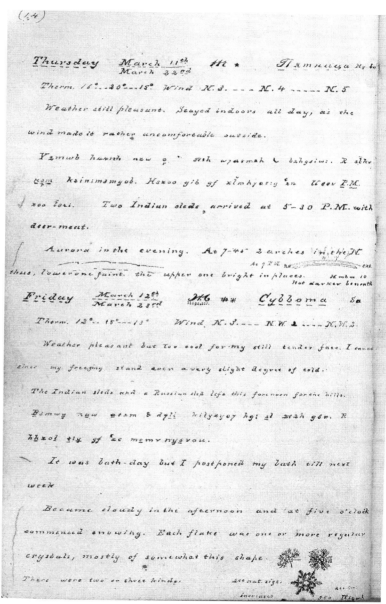

Page from Bannister's diary showing words in Cyrillic and in code.

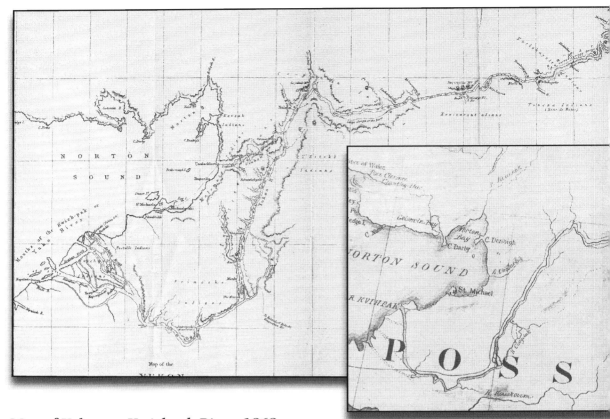

Map of Yukon or Kwichpak River, 1868

The undated map above was included with Whymper's book, *Travels and Adventures in Russian America,* published in 1868. The map's legend explains that the multiple mouths of the Yukon River delta have been furnished by Western Union. The lower course of the river up to the Great Bend and slightly beyond is taken from Zakoskin's map. Credit for mapping the rest of the river is given to the artist Fredrick Whymper who, with William Dall, ascended the Yukon from Nulato to Fort Yukon and then descended the full length from Fort Yukon to St. Michael's. His charting places Fort Yukon well north of its position on the center map.

Map of Proposed Route of Collins Overland Telegraph, Western Union Extension

The center map shows the information available to the members of the Yukon party when they began planning a path for the telegraph line in 1865. The lower course of the river was clearly mapped and some tributaries were included. The Ulukak River connecting the coast with the Yukon River was indicated and the Great Bend of the river was plotted. But the telegraph line was planned to follow the course of the river from Fort Yukon to the Great Bend and that area of the river was marked "Unexplored," represented by an artistic squiggle. Neither the land nor the river had been mapped.

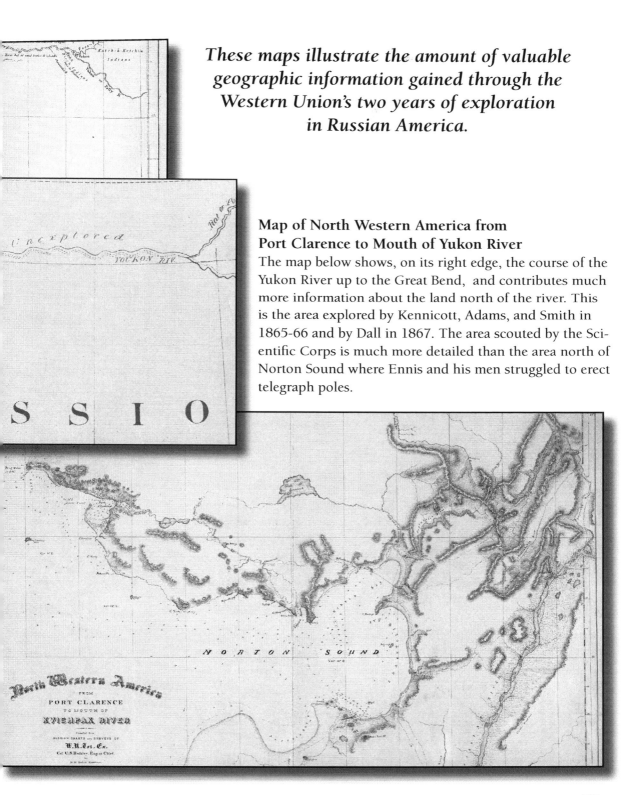

These maps illustrate the amount of valuable geographic information gained through the Western Union's two years of exploration in Russian America.

Map of North Western America from Port Clarence to Mouth of Yukon River

The map below shows, on its right edge, the course of the Yukon River up to the Great Bend, and contributes much more information about the land north of the river. This is the area explored by Kennicott, Adams, and Smith in 1865-66 and by Dall in 1867. The area scouted by the Scientific Corps is much more detailed than the area north of Norton Sound where Ennis and his men struggled to erect telegraph poles.

Unalacleet and Nulato
Winter 1865-66

For a man with a self-acknowledged history of depression since his teens, Kennicott could not have come to the Far North at a worse time of year. He often felt lethargic in the short gray days of winter but felt awake and alive as spring came. His original plan of arriving in June would have meant twenty-one daylight hours in which he could work happily. The approaching winter would reduce the Land of the Midnight Sun to less than four hours of daylight each day in the area he was to explore. Through the darkening October days at Unalacleet, Kennicott arranged for housing, hired an interpreter, and bargained for dog sleds to take his group on to Fort Nulato.

Unalacleet, a much smaller fort than St. Michael's, only twenty-six feet by fifteen feet, had no space for either extra supplies or men. Because the weather rapidly turned colder, the first task of the Western Union men was to build a rudimentary home for themselves. Using drift logs about a foot in diameter, they improved two existing fish houses the Russians had built against the outside walls of the fort. One house, about ten feet square, they used for cooking and dining; the other, about fourteen feet by twenty feet, they used for sleeping and storage. They banked the walls with sod and gravel, chinked the logs with moss, and added an essential chimney, the mortar for which was made with mud and boiling water.

The log house was "a very hastily built affair and therefore imperfect, a little too airy for one thing." Since Unalacleet means "place where the east wind blows," the house's airiness was probably understated by Bannister. "During the nights the air within was not as a general thing much above zero and very often considerably below that point. The house was nevertheless quite a comfortable place. It had a nice large fireplace which made the room very cheerful looking, and we kept tolerably warm by using plenty of fuel."[1] However "the windows did not, as at St. Michael's aspire to the dignity of glass, but were of the gut of fur seal, white and translucent, if not transparent."[2] It was not a place to linger, and no one was assigned to stay there. But when the men visited, the rooms were better than being outside.

From time to time, supplies were brought from St. Michael's to Unalacleet where they would then be transported to Ennis's group as they explored around Norton Sound or to Kennicott's group as they investigated the Nulato area. As a result, Bannister reported the men "lived here fully as well as at St. Michaels, though in a somewhat rougher style. Reindeer meat and trout were abundant, besides our regular provisions, such as flour, pilot bread [hard tack], bacon, etc., with such luxuries as preserved fruits, and plenty of sugar and tea."[3] But Bannister visited Unalacleet only once, in the early months of the expedition, when all supplies seemed sufficient.

While Pease went with the initial group transferring supplies to Unalacleet, he did not go with Kennicott to Nulato. Kennicott was now effectively alone. None of the men going with him to Nulato knew him from previous years; they were not his friends or fellow scientists but rather were explorers under his command. In addition, Nulato, the place they would stay for months, had an unnerving connection to one of the most haunting stories of the Far North: the Franklin Expedition's search for the Northwest Passage.

The search for a sea passage across the top of the American continent had attracted the Western world for hundreds of years. But the most compelling and absorbing search was for one of the expeditions, lost in the ice. From 1845 when Sir John Franklin organized his elaborate expedition until all hope of finding him and his men was given up in 1859, newspapers and magazines focused on him, his goals, and the multiple searches for him. The drama of his expedition — and the decade of hopeful searching — centered on the same section of the globe as did the Western Union Telegraph Expedition. While no one knew with certainty why Franklin's expedition had never returned, everyone read the descriptions of the snow-covered wasteland, the life-threatening weather conditions, and the ship-crushing ice that his expedition, and those searching for him, had to overcome. Kennicott's men would have known the Franklin story well.

In 1865, when the Western Union Expedition was signing on men, the fate of Franklin and the trials of the various search expe-

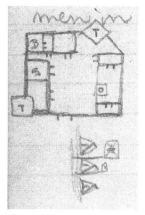

Unlabeled fort in Dall's diary. From context, almost certainly Unalacleet.

ditions had to have been fresh in most men's minds even as they agreed to work in that same climate. Kennicott referred to those previous expeditions when he bragged that the men he had hired were so good he would "bet on them to discover the open polar sea."[4] As a further reminder of Franklin's fate, Plover Bay in Siberia, one of the stops on the Western Union ships' route, was named for the HMS *Plover* whose party overwintered there in 1848-49 while searching for Franklin. A search party also stopped at St. Michael's and a group headed by Lt. John Bernard of the British Royal Navy went up to Fort Nulato to ask about Franklin. Natives there attacked the fort and killed Bernard in 1851. Now Kennicott and his men would meet the same tribe, stay in the same fort, and pass by Bernard's grave daily.

But Kennicott's group could not leave for Nulato just yet. Even though sunlight decreased day by day and the temperature fell below freezing, the swampy land they had to cross just on the other side of the hills around Unalacleet was not yet frozen solid. Adams, sent out to explore by boat early in October, reported large blocks of ice in the river and temperatures so cold that his paddle became so heavily coated with ice that he could hardly lift it. But it still was not cold enough.

Finally, at the end of October, with less than eight hours of daylight and temperatures about sixteen degrees below zero, the swamp was safely frozen. Without dog sleds, Smith, Adams, Lebarge, two Russians and two Indians left on foot with Kennicott for Nulato, a distance of about 110 miles.[5] All of them, except Kennicott, carried heavy packs, another lapse that caused his men to comment. On the trail a week later, Adams humorously noted, "the Indians seem to be living on nothing, which is cheap living and does not take much trouble to digest."[6] But since Kennicott had counted on buying food from those same now-starving natives, their situation quickly affected him and his men. The very next day, they "took a light breakfast on the recollection of what we had eaten the day before."[7]

Besides very short rations and little daylight, they were exploring through a fog, a frozen mist, an endless grayness. When they finally reached the clifflike banks of the Yukon River south of Nulato, the grayness became a vast expanse of ice and an unlimited, monotonous landscape of hills and trees almost indistinguishable from one another. From here, they traveled on the mile-wide river whose relatively flat ice made the trip a little easier and somewhat faster. When they reached Nulato on November 9, after ten days on the trail, their faces were iced over, their cheeks and noses frostbitten.

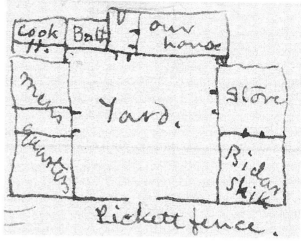

Nulato's isolated, inaccessible location and its garrison of just three men caused the Russians, many of whom were prisoners, to scorn it as solitary confinement. Fort Nulato was located on the west bank of the Yukon River even though the river itself flows generally from east to west. But just above Nulato the Yukon interrupts its straight rush to the ocean and, with an elbow turn, flows almost due south; its banks then are on the east and west. The fort, oriented north-south, about one hundred feet on a side, and set back about fifty feet from the Yukon, was the standard Russian model built of logs, with the commander's house at a corner near the entrance. "The fort is composed of five or six buildings in the shape of a quadrangle consisting of the bidershik's [commander's] house; two stores [warehouses] one above the other where goods and furs are kept; our house, formerly a store house; a bath house; a cookhouse; and the 'casame' or barracks for rabbotniks or workmen, and two small towers above in each of which is a small cannon."[8] Nulato would be their home for as long as it took to find a path for the telegraph wire from the Great Bend in the Yukon River to the northern coast of Norton Sound. The high hills that edged the river causing it to turn south would have to be penetrated. But again, there were food and housing to arrange first.

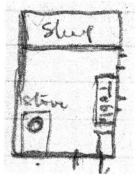

Above: Plan of Fort Nulato.
Below: Plan of room used by WU men at Nulato.

The Russians at the fort were willing to convert a twenty foot by thirty foot fur storeroom into Western Union living quarters for two hundred and fifty rubles, about fifty dollars. The room, in the northwest corner of the fort, held a sleeping platform at one twenty-foot end that provided minimal comfort for the men who slept in a row. At best, it raised the men off an equally hard floor that could be as much as sixty degrees colder than the upper parts of the room. Two windows, once again of split seal intestines, faced the courtyard and admitted the light but not the view. A fireplace to the right of the door served for cooking; a traditional Russian stove may have heated the room. Although there was enough space for Kennicott, Ketchum, Lebarge, Adams, and Smith, privacy would have been rare.

The Russians would share their fort, but they were not willing to share their meager stores. Their food supplies had to last for not just the winter months, but through the early spring months and into June when the barges from St. Michael's could safely get up the huge river with replenishments. Kennicott understood their reluctance but had few options himself. There was effectively no hunting to be done; the game was gone long ago into the hills. Fishing was possible, but the catch was minimal. The foodstuffs at St. Michael's, already far less than Kennicott had originally requested, must be shared with the Norton Sound group. Now that he could see the conditions he faced, Kennicott returned almost immediately to Unalacleet and went on to St. Michael's by December 2 for supplies and advice.

When the dogs he had requested arrived, Kennicott set off for Unalacleet with Bannister on December 10, 1865. As Bannister observed, "There is very little pleasure in winter traveling in this region, when you have the best of dogs and good weather; you cannot sit on the sled but must run or freeze. The only time you enjoy yourself is when you come into camp at night, change your clothing, which is generally wet through with perspiration or melting snow, drink about a quart of hot tea, and have a nice warm meal before you. The remembrance of the former misery makes one appreciate the slightest comforts. The case is still worse when the dogs are poor and the roads [sled trails] bad as was the case with us."[9] Yet, since the end of October, Kennicott had been traveling almost nonstop.

Bannister and Kennicott joined Adams, Ennis, Smith, Chappell, Cotter, Bendeleben, and Denison to spend Christmas in Unalacleet's log houses. Their three-hour day lasted from sunrise at 10:45 in the morning to sunset at 1:45 in the afternoon. In the evenings, they gathered close around a large log fire to sing songs and talk of home. Because the wool uniforms purchased in San Francisco were too thin for the Arctic climate, they had all bought Eskimo clothing at their own expense and looked like natives dressed in skins and furs. Bannister found the native footwear much superior to his leather boots: for the first time in his life, his feet were warm in the winter. Before New Year's, Kennicott went back to Nulato

Parka style worn by native men.

while Bannister and Bendeleben returned to St. Michael's traveling on the ice of the sound that had frozen to a very safe depth of about five feet.

Bannister's description of that trip from fort to fort clearly illustrates the problems of winter travel in the Yukon. "I left Unalakleet on the 30th of December....The second day of the journey was very cold and shortly after we had started the wind sprang up....The wind soon increased to a perfect gale and though the shore was very near we could see it only once in a while through the driving snow....We moved very slowly; and all of us either pulling or pushing on the sled. I remember thawing my nose nine times and my cheeks several times but at the tenth trial Jack Frost got the best of me, and I found that no amount of rubbing...would bring out the frost....before long my face swelled so much that my eyes were nearly closed and I was obliged to fall behind. I lost sight of the sled entirely at a point two miles from...our destination, not being able to see more than two rods ahead. I feared most of all missing my way and going too far out to sea which would bring me past the village. In that case my fate was certain, for I might wander all night or until I gave it up exhausted....I was walking along shore when I met with an Eskimo...who had been sent out to find me. He took me directly to the village where I thawed out with cold water....I stayed with the natives till the next day....At St. Michael's I was well cared for and was almost entirely well in two weeks, though I could not endure any severe cold for the rest of the winter. Mr. Bendeleben, my fellow traveler, lost a part of his ear.[10] According to Dall, Bannister nearly died. During that winter the lowest temperature recorded on the shore was fifty-four degrees below zero; the heaviest snowfall added two feet to the base amount.

The weather was only one of the expedition's problems. The Russians at St. Michael's had assured Kennicott it was possible to purchase fish and other foodstuffs from native villages along the bank of the Yukon. Instead, Kennicott found that the nomadic Indians routinely moved inland away from the river during the winter, following the large game into the mountains. Their riverside villages of the summer were empty. Kennicott now became even more dependent on the generosity of the Russians and on the Western Union supplies at Unalacleet. But distributing those supplies by dogsled proved difficult because there was not enough frozen black fish to feed the ever-hungry dogs, the sled loads were extra heavy, and the snow was softer than the Russians had said it would be.

The first week of January, 1866, they bought "four new light Ingerlick sleighs good for going on the ice but very bad for the portage."[11] The Ingerlick sleds were ten or twelve feet long with a birch framework so light that any piece except the runners could be easily broken with two hands. When the pieces were all lashed together, the sled was strong enough to hold five or six hundred pounds yet it bent like a bow going around a corner or over a log.

Kennicott continued to explore the area, determined both to reach the eastern Fort Yukon and to find a short route overland from Nulato west to Norton Sound. He and the Norton Sound explorers agreed not to meet until the Western Union ships came in the summer, but they were in constant communication, sending Indian couriers with multipage letters to keep each other informed about their progress and problems. For example, Ennis, on the coast, knew how Adams, exploring out of Nulato, had climbed a high mount and saw that "Continual ranges of mountains covered the country as far as the eye could see and the prospect then looked gloomy enough to find an available pass for telegraph purposes."[12]

Adams, however, was usually able to bring some humor to his diary: "This was the fifth time my nose has frozen today. I also froze my finger, cheek, and toe. I begin to think it is getting cold."[13] The temperature that day, the end of January 1866, was fifty-eight degrees below zero at Nulato.

Arriving by dogsled at the mile-wide frozen Yukon River.

Trust but Verify
2005

I was absolutely determined to see Adams's diary in its handwritten form, not just its book form, *Life on the Yukon, 1865–1867*. Having been blindsided by the absence of coded passages in Bannister's published diary, I sheepishly remembered the first injunction given every sleuth: trust no one. OK, trust, but verify.

Encouragingly, the same library held both Adams's diary and the never-published holograph diary of Smith. I considered Fred Smith and George Adams probably the most accurate and unbiased of the diarists because neither of them had any connections with Kennicott, his family, or the Smithsonian Institution. They had no vested interest in the science of the expedition; their only job was to help Kennicott in his explorations. I trusted these two to describe events as they happened.

I was having so much trouble piecing together bits of information from them and from the other widely separated sources that I really didn't need the two libraries I used at the Smithsonian's Natural History museum to mess with my mind the way they did.

It seemed to me that the John Wesley Powell Library of Anthropology, where I read Bannister's and Adams's published diaries, kept changing its location without moving a book. If I used the operator-run elevators to reach the library, I asked for the third floor. If I used the staff self-service elevator, I stepped off on the sixth floor. Where, really, was I?

Then, the main library on the ground floor of the Natural History museum left me in midair. I came to read Smith's and Adams's diaries using microfilm readers on the library's second floor. The readers were neatly lined up sideways at the window wall and I deliberately chose a reader at a window space rather than a wall space so I could rest my eyes by looking out onto the street. I failed to notice that the floor wasn't attached to anything at my side: the floor ended, then there was a space, then there was the window glass. Instead of anything solid immediately at my elbow, there was air. Low railings of small pipes, one at my knee, one at my ankle, kept me on the second floor. Anything I dropped might land on the first floor. The library's two floors had been fitted into the same height as the vaulted ceiling of the elegant entrance lobby so the tall windows didn't stop at the first floor ceiling but stopped about midway up the second floor wall. I was ungrounded, exactly the way my research made me feel.

I spent hours and hours puzzling over

the penmanship of two men who fought the Yukon every day just to stay alive. They described an experience so uncommon I could barely picture it. Turning off the microfilm reader and pulling myself out of an icebound nineteenth-century expedition only to find myself afloat in a twenty-first-century library required an extra moment or two to get my bearings.

Each diary held its own surprise. I was hoping Smith would add more information about Kennicott's death and the treatment of his body. Instead, several diary pages after his death were missing, torn out long ago. But, in Adams's diary I found the biggest — and best — surprise. In the margin of a page, Adams drew the marks Kennicott made in the river beach just before he died. Although the drawing was missing from the published book, the editor left a space in the text to show something had been omitted — as if, almost, to encourage searching for the drawing. Here, now, in front of me, was the essential information I needed!

If I ever questioned the researcher's injunction to see original documents, the diaries of the Yukon explorers gave me the answer.

Another "trust but verify" event happened by accident.

I'd been told Kennicott's body couldn't have been transferred in San Francisco from the wooden casket made in Nulato to the metal one exhumed in Illinois because metal caskets weren't available in California in 1866. At that time, most metal caskets were manufactured in Ohio and shipped from there to other cities. Everyone knew it would have been too difficult and too expensive to ship such items to California.

Not that I doubted my informants, but I'd exhausted the microfilmed newspaper sources I'd come to the Library of Congress to check, and, looking around for something else to search, I noticed file cabinets full of city directories near me. The microfilmed San Francisco city directory from 1866 was right there; it would only take a minute to look for funeral parlors.

Not only were seven funeral parlors in town, but three were on the same street, and one of them advertised the newest and most effective of metal caskets. Assuming America's entrepreneurial, competitive spirit operated then as now, it was a fair bet that other parlors sold them, too. It would have been not only possible, but downright easy, for Kennicott's body to be transferred from a battered wood casket in San Francisco, where his friends had more time to make the arrangements than anywhere else.

Trust, but verify.

I was beginning to wonder if I could trust Kennicott's own words.

Nulato
Winter 1866

" **I**'m in a state of profound coma out of which I only arouse to become the prey of 40,000 blue D__ls [devils]….I only awaken to become low spirited enough to cut my throat as I think I might do if anyone else could attend to matters at Nuklukai'it and Ft. Youkon for me. — These continued obstacles and delays nearly drive me mad. I'd rather be in a tread mill."[1]

In the middle of February 1866, Kennicott described his mental state in letters to his men at Unalacleet and at St. Michael's. The scant daylight, now about five hours daily, along with the increasing cold and snow made it harder and harder for him to function well. Yet, despite his mental condition, he pushed himself physically just as he had on his previous trip to the Far North. For Ken-

Interior of Fort Nulato with aurora; probably showing, at the back, the room used by WU men.

nicott, life at Nulato since January had become an intense exploration of the hills north and west of the fort. Kennicott was also determined to go east to Fort Yukon, a personal goal of his since Bulkley had said that exploration of the Upper Yukon could wait until his return the next spring.

Adams, Smith, and Lebarge shuttled between Nulato and Unalacleet bringing supplies by dogsled. For one dinner on the trail Adams "examined our provision bag and found we had nothing to eat except a little flour, three tallow candles and some tea. We were very hungry, had had nothing to eat since morning so we melted the candles and made slapjacks and they were as good to us with our appetites as if they had been fried in fresh California butter. Persons who have not had experience here cannot imagine what a terrific appetite a person gets here in winter."[2] At another trail meal they broke a hatchet hacking at a frozen loaf of bread, understanding too late why the Russians sliced fresh bread and toasted it before packing it along on the trail.

There was much more they all learned too late. Critically, the Nulato Indians professed to know nothing about the surrounding countryside and refused to guide them into the hills because that was Malamute country, the guarded territory of a rival tribe. Even Kennicott, who had always received the help and cooperation of natives, was surprised by "the unwillingness of the Indians to have us enter this region never before visited by white men."[3] Yet Kennicott persisted. He wrote of taking a fifteen-day reconnaissance up the Yukon in the first days of February. Then the weather warmed, thawing the snow, and he had to wait to begin his next exploration. Still, Kennicott finished out the month with a three-day exploration of nearby mountains.

Kennicott was still planning to reach Fort Yukon in the winter. In part, his plans were based on the projections he had made back in San Francisco for the Fraser River exploration group. If Pope and Rothrock were able to follow his plan, they would be at Fort Yukon by March or April and he wanted to be there to greet them. What Kennicott could not know was that, in February, as he felt totally frustrated about his own plans, the Fraser River explorers were still south of Babine Lake, less than a quarter of the way to Fort Yukon.

Kennicott faced his own obstacles in reaching Fort Yukon. Getting there under any conditions would be a huge and hazardous undertaking. It was calculated to be five hundred miles away by uncharted river and an unknown number of miles away over an unexplored land of hills, rivers, and forests. He wrote Ennis, "I do not feel at all sure of reaching Fort Youkon on snow shoes. I'm determined to try, however, and shall leave here on the final start as early in March as the snow begins to harden — or certainly before the 15th possibly by the 1st to 5th — somewhat dependant on the reception of dry fish and oil from Unalachleet."[4]

Snowshoes make winter travel possible by holding the wearer up in the top three or four inches of snow. The snowshoes used at Nulato measured 64 inches long, 5 inches wide, with an upward curve at the toe of 11 inches, and were made of thinly shaved hard wood covered in dried, furred, seal skin.[5] To walk, a wearer must lift his feet out of the snow or slide through it, making the condition of the snow critical. When the snow is soft, the snowshoer sinks further into it, making the next step a very high one. When the snow is wet, it clings to the snowshoes, adding extra pounds to every step, exhausting the wearer. Kennicott had to wait until the snow compacted or developed an icy crust from daytime melting and nighttime freezing. He also had to wait for foodstuffs from Unalacleet.

Supplying Nulato from Unalacleet had become much more difficult because of an annually recurring disease resembling rabies that killed their dogs. On March 7, 1866, when Smith returned from Unalacleet with his dogsled of provisions, Kennicott despaired. "The sight of Smith's [sickly] dogs gave the death blow to any lingering hope of starting up the Youkon with any large party...." he wrote to the coastal explorers. "My last hope died hard, took a whole day to flicker out in — but the Youkon winter expedition is dead now. This morning I felt somewhat as I remembered to have felt the morning I awoke after my father's death. I think, Ennis, you can understand and fully appreciate what I must have suffered in seeing my hopes drop one by one ever since about the time you left here. Good bye winter trip to Ft. Youkon!...."[6] Kennicott then drew in his letter a cracked tombstone labeled 'Youkon' in overgrown grass.

Kennicott's difficult decision may have been a relief to his men. Adams confessed, "It has been for some time back apparent to us all that an exploration to Fort Yukon in winter is impossible and if tried would most certainly be attended with loss of life. The

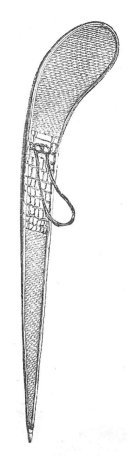

Kennicott's compass with his initials scratched into the cover.

snow is soft and does not get as hard as represented by the Russians and it would be impossible to get through it at the rate we would have to go with loaded sleds even if we had the dogs. Out of sixteen dogs, all we have left at this place are but nine that are fit to go on a short trip and none capable of making such a trip as we have contemplated. So the winter Expedition to the English Redout [Fort Yukon] has to be given up. It has been decided to go back to Unalaclet and bring over on sleds a Bidaraw and Bidock & provisions and be ready at the first open water to start for F.Y. [Fort Yukon.]"[7]

A *biadara* was the Russian name for an open boat, thirty-five long and six feet wide at the top, slightly narrower at the flat bottom, but much narrower at each pointed end. Small sticks woven together made little racks to keep the contents away from the bottom of the boat. To speed travel, a square sail could be rigged from a center pole. A *baidarka*, or small boat, was a light canoe, similar to a kayak but with watertight places for three passengers. Both boats were made of a sewn patchwork of thick, tough, oiled seal skin stretched over a light framework of birch wood fastened together with sinews.

Smith, Adams, Ketchum, and Lebarge started off the next day for Unalacleet, leaving Kennicott with the Russians and natives to make more explorations of the mountains around Nulato. During this time, Kennicott wrote lengthy letters. To Ennis he insisted, "Under existing circumstances, however, you will not send any of your party to start from here. I can with difficulty find means to subsist those gentlemen retained in this division...." Specifically, Kennicott explained, "Very few fish are being caught here now — No deer near and the partridges have all gone so that in order to secure the Youkon Exped, I have to be very economical of provisions....I confess with considerable mortification that my favorite Youkon is not the land flowing with milk and honey – otherwise deer tongue and moose backfat....I find these D___d Koyukons [natives] live on martens [sables], rabbits and blackfish... all winter; except when they catch fish about here. This, however, has been an unusually hard year."[8] Kennicott did sound a positive note: they would not have known how barren the country was if the steamer had not failed and forced them to explore over land in the winter.

Then he received a letter from Ennis that brightened his prospects. Ennis strongly suggested that coastal natives used a trail through the mountains to hunt for game inland, knowledge Kennicott had not received when he first questioned the Nulato natives. Using this new information, Kennicott confronted the local natives and closely questioned them. They not only confirmed Ennis's information, but also admitted knowing of a river route northwest of Nulato that led the whole distance west to the sea. Kennicott, who had benefitted from his interchanges years earlier with British American natives, was forced to acknowledge his misplaced trust in these natives. He admitted he was "growing very wary in believing the statements of these rascally Koyukons."[9] After complimenting Ennis for putting "an entirely new face on the aspect of affairs," Kennicott wrote fourteen pages of his exploration plans, rough charts of the area, and as full descriptions, including compass points, as he could about how to get to Nulato from Norton Sound. Once again upbeat, he even said that giving up his cherished Yukon trip was for the best because it allowed him to find this path for the telegraph wire.[10]

One of two maps by Kennicott giving specific directions and showing the route overland from Nulato to Norton Sound. This, Chart No. 2, focuses on the Nulato area.

Two of Ennis's men, Dyer and Cotter, were going to try to reach Nulato from the coast over the route Kennicott had mapped. Kennicott again wrote about the conditions: "Indians have found no deer and been starved out....For god's sake don't let Dyer and Cotter go into that region without provisions enough to enable them to turn back...."[11] And he added his basic creed: "Better to expend something in needless energy than to risk failure by want of forethought."[12]

At the same time, he told the men at St. Michael's of the situation. "This country is a damnable one at all times and this is a starvation year; no deer, no fish....But the things brought across the [swamp] at cost of so much sweating and swearing now secure us till spring....Should Bannister feel very anxious for more Arctic experiences, let him get...some of the old dogfish and live on it a few days sleeping meantime on a hillside with a single blanket....If ever you get to feeling dull or melancholy…just imagine the state of my mind and let the comparison help to make you more contented....I shall notify Col. Bulkley of my resignation of all authority upon his arrival...."[13]

Winter was now ending, minute by sunlit minute. The darkest days of late December and January were now stretching toward a more pleasant ten hours of sunlight. Kennicott was only too aware of the coming spring and his long-abandoned commitment to collect museum specimens. Up to this time he had not mentioned collecting any natural history materials but now he noted: "No Natural History work on the coast and I obliged to leave here [Nulato] at the very time I might make good collections...."[14] He wrote a short note on March 21 asking Pease to compensate. "You will now have a good chance at natural history. Pray pile in and do all you can. You could not be in a better place than Norton Sound for doing good. You can do a great deal by teaching the Indians to collect. Get them to get seals no matter if not fine skins. ...Go in and do your best Charlie — I shall take my whack next spring."[15] In a slightly more formal way, he urged the same task onto Ennis: "I need scarcely tell you how very much obliged I will be by any collections in Natural History that you can make for the Smithsonian Institution....an outfit of only a few pounds weight would enable any parties...to make highly creditable additions to the scientific knowledge of this almost unknown region....You can hardly go wrong in collecting almost anything and you can very likely do a great deal by inducing the Indians to collect specimens and to bring them in fall to Unalakhleet."[16]

At the same time, Kennicott wrote one more letter: to the commander of Fort Yukon asking him to wait for Kennicott's arrival at an informal fur trading post about halfway between Nulato and Fort Yukon. "I hope to be at Nuklukai'it (the mouth of the 'Big River') on my way to Ft. Youkon...about June 15th possibly earlier. It is called 15 days in canoe from here to Nuklukai'it and the same from there to Ft. Youkon." Kennicott gave as his address, "Russian Fur Co's Post Nulato, Kuikpak (Youkon) River (about 500 miles above sea and supposed to be the same below Ft. Youkon)"[17]

With his obligations to natural history taken care of, and his projected plans in mind, Kennicott continued his explorations of the Nulato area expecting to be gone from about March 25 to April 5. On one of only sixteen pages of his notes remaining from the Western Union expedition, Kennicott wrote:

"Mar. 24 — 20 degrees below zero

Mar. 31 — Stopped at old camp... [guide] Sedorka too blind [with snow blindness] to go on. I nearly as bad and obliged to walk behind — the snow growing soft decided to sleep a while and carry on at night.

Apr. 1st — watch stopped [Kennicott multiplied the length of his paces by the number per minute and the time he had been walking to know how far he had traveled.]

Apr. 2nd — to fort"[18]

He told Ketchum and others after his return that he had been out of his head while on the mountains. Still, Kennicott kept exploring the area, going on April 18 with Adams, two Indians, a sled and five dogs to a tributary of the Yukon. There were now more than eighteen hours of daylight.

On the evening of the April 12, the men enjoyed a very pleasant evening "and we were out in front of the fort singing for some time. The days are very long now; the sun rises before three in the morning and sets after nine. At the fort we go to bed before dark and do not get up until long after sunrise. Now it is just eleven P.M. and light as day."[19] These were the kinds of days that, on his previous northern expedition, awoke Kennicott from his torpor and restored him to full vitality. The additional sunlight and the approaching spring then gave him energy to work ceaselessly. Any depression he might have had lifted and he attacked his tasks with vigor.

Kennicott may also have been cheered by the arrival at Nulato of his old friend, Pease. For the previous seven months Pease had worked along the coast with Ennis and his men and no one explains why Pease now made the ten-day trek to Nulato. At this time, through Pease or some other source, Kennicott learned that Ennis had officially recorded, "If there had not been so much humbugging and foolishness on the part of our commander [Kennicott], we should have been at Fort Youkon long ago, and I shall report so to Col. Bulkley."[20]

Ennis had been chosen by Kennicott to take over if anything

happened to him. In addition, Kennicott had obviously thought of Ennis as a friend, writing long letters to him explaining the conditions he faced and revealing his feelings of despair. Ennis received many letters in which Kennicott agonized over the best approach to use to reach Fort Yukon. Kennicott regularly wrote about the various choices he might make. If one thing happened, he would do *this*; but he might do *that*; unless, of course, it became possible to do *yet another*. Kennicott's "thinking out loud" in the letters gave the appearance of not being able to make up his mind. In some cases, Kennicott did seem to delay unnecessarily. He would write of leaving to explore "the next day" but then not actually leave for a week. The timing of his treks often depended on things beyond his control, such as the snow freezing or the supplies arriving. Yet, to military-minded men, Kennicott's flexibility may have been unusual enough to be called humbugging. Bannister acknowledged this attitude toward Kennicott in his diary code after The Major's death: "No one is his enemy now!" Evidently, Kennicott did have enemies, known to him or not, while he lived.

Kennicott's own men were also troubled by his behavior. On April 22, 1866, just when Pease arrived, Smith expressed his contempt: "Mr. Kennicott has made another change in his plans (nothing unusual.) I am to go with him to Fort Youkon, and Ketchum and Pease to go down the river to explore that portion. He also

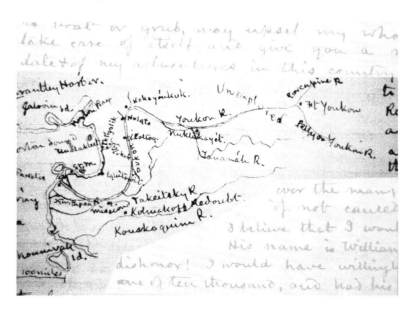

Map sketch showing the unexplored area.

said that he might want to send me on from there [Fort Yukon] and again might send me back to the ship to report while he went on. I don't know what to make of this man; I begin to think he is crazy, he has succeeded in making himself generally disagreeable and has disgusted us all to such an extent that hardly one will remain in the country another year, at least to be in any way connected with him."[21] Almost a year earlier in San Francisco, Dall had made a similar observation.

Crazy or not, Kennicott's skills and abilities now allowed Cotter and Dyer to find the mountain path Kennicott had drawn and described. They arrived at Nulato from the coast on April 27, successfully completing a possible route for the telegraph line. During that same week, all of the Nulato men returned from Unalacleet with the two large sealskin boats and additional provisions. While the others made preparations to go up the Yukon in the canoes as soon as the ice left the river, Adams was sent to explore a nearby Yukon tributary as a possible path for the telegraph line and left on April 28.

It was now approaching the longest days of the year, when Smith and Kennicott could write at a table inside their room near midnight and still be in what Smith considered broad daylight. That same sunlight raised the temperature so high that the snow did not freeze at night, making Adams's travel by dogsled through watery snow impossibly slow. Defeated, he returned to Nulato by May 10, 1866. The Yukon River was thawing rapidly and in front of the fort was free of ice almost halfway across. The Nulato and a smaller river north of the fort were both ice free. Geese had returned to the island in front of the fort where Pease, Smith and the Russians went to shoot them.

Fort Nulato sited on a bluff with, perhaps, steps leading to the Yukon River.

Russian Rescue 2004

The men's expeditions to shoot geese on the island across from the fort were exercises in danger, and Kennicott was part of a dramatic rescue in the Yukon River.

As Smith and Adams tell it, the incident happened in the morning of May 12, 1866. Sections of the Yukon River were open but the ice still held tight to islands directly across from Nulato. The Nulato men, tired of the skimpy meals of winter, were eager enough for fresh food to risk the ice, the debris, and the roaring river itself. Pease and Smith went on May 11 and came back safely with geese. A Russian, trying the same adventure the next day, wasn't as skillful or as lucky. On his way back from the island, the ice broke free, punctured his birch bark canoe, and he began to sink. He was near the shore but still far enough away to be in great danger.

From the fort parapet where they were walking, Ketchum and Dyer saw the man up to his chin in the river and called others from the fort to launch canoes to rescue the Russian. "In an instant–almost–our two Malymuts had got our baidara into the water and were off after him. The Baiderjuk [fort commander] also going out in a canoe. By using a paddle between the canoe and baidara, he was enabled to get into the baidara and he came ashore alright only minus his gun and canoe."[1] When everyone was safely ashore, Kennicott rewarded the Russian rescuers' bravery and quick action.

Dall tells the story differently in *Transactions*, giving Kennicott direct credit for the dramatic rescue. "The Major was walking on the roof of the barracks and saw [the Russian's] danger. In a moment he had launched another canoe, and with an Indian forced his way through the blocks of heaving ice, rescuing the Russian in the nick of time."[2] Having lived at the fort, Dall surely knew how long it would take to get down from the parapet, out of the fort, and down the bluff to the water line, making his version less likely.

Perhaps, as the story was probably repeated over and over in the months before Dall had a chance to hear it, the names just got switched from Ketchum to Kennicott, and Dall wrote the story as he was told it. Even if Dall knew the accurate version, his story correctly reflects Kennicott's characteristic kindness and concern for others.

Lead and Arsenic
2010

When the chemical analyses of Kennicott's remains came back, small amounts of arsenic and exceptionally high amounts of lead were found in his body. Why were those poisonous chemicals there at all? I hoped to find an answer in the reference library of the Smithsonian's National Museum of American History.

American History was closed for renovation at the time. Closed to the public, that is. Staff, workmen, and researchers could still use the entrance underneath the Mall, in a narrow driveway tunnel designed for deliveries. Alert to both the puddles on the driveway and the pigeons on the rafters, I entered the small doorway. There, security personnel checked badges and monitored sign-in sheets, all under a white glare of many lights. The ground floor museum area, however, was startlingly quiet, really dark after the bright lights, and totally unfamiliar. My arms tightened around my notebook. To clear the museum for the extensive renovation, exhibits had been moved in their entirety to the ground floor. Case after case, each one taller than me, stood in what had become a large holding area. In the silent dimness, I was alone among them. I breathed more rapidly. One narrow, uncluttered path, marked off by the stanchions-and-straps used for crowd control, wove through the cases. Above it, widely spaced work lights glowed rather than illuminated. Beyond my actual footpath the rest of the area was in shadowy darkness. My step quickened.

The tall display cases were wrapped in clear plastic sheeting lightly bound with wide blue tape. They looked strangled, but they breathed, the plastic sheeting moving slightly, going in and out with soft sounds. Worse, short blips of light winked from unexpected places. By the time my eyes flicked to the light flash, it was gone.

Just then, a concealed-by-the-cases workman appeared almost in front of me and I jerked sideways, involuntarily. It took all the intellectualizing I could muster to tell my spooked senses that air must be moving the plastic that then reflected the dim work lights. Air currents. Air currents.

My shoulders finally relaxed in the brightly lit elevator up to the fifth floor reference library where I would focus on the killer poisons of arsenic and lead.

One ounce of lead, in the form of lead acetate, was listed in the expedition's medical supplies in 1866 but a much shorter list of medicines recorded by Bannister at St. Michael's in 1865 doesn't include lead acetate. The medicine couldn't have been taken to Nulato by Kennicott and lead in any form was never listed in the scientific supplies. Yet, there was lead in Kennicott's body.

In fact, there was so much lead in Kennicott's remains at the time of his autopsy (111 micrograms per gram in his nail; 636 micrograms per gram in his stomach) that if it had been present at those levels in life he would have had noticeable symptoms such as blackened teeth, severe stomach cramps, and significant muscle weakness. The surprisingly large quantity of lead in his hair, 5,813 micrograms per gram, was "at least one order of magnitude beyond the highest values that hair can reach from endogenous sources [sources within the body]."[1] The amount of lead found at autopsy couldn't have been in Kennicott's body during life.

Ground water entered both the wood coffin and the metal casket, dissolving and distributing lead to Kennicott's remains. If the boards from the fort had been painted, lead could have leached from the wood into the coffin made in Nulato. Metal caskets like Kennicott's were commonly covered both inside and out with lead paint, although no paint was found on his heavily rusted casket at the autopsy. The lead seal on the metal casket was eliminated as a source because the isotopes of the coffin seal and the lead in Kennicott's remains were not the same.

Another possible source, lead acetate crystals, also called sugar of lead for their appearance and sweet taste, have been used for centuries. Lead acetate was known to be fatal in large doses whether it was swallowed, inhaled, or simply ab-

sorbed through the skin. In smaller doses, usually combined with opium, it was used regularly by nineteenth-century doctors because its astringent quality stopped bleeding both in internal hemorrhages and in surface burns or large cuts. It was also recognized as an effective insecticide that could have been used to protect the furs warehoused at Nulato.

If they had lead acetate, the men at Nulato might have sprinkled the crystals on Kennicott's body to kill insects, or they might have used a lead wash on his body as many funeral parlors did at the time. A mortician dealing with Kennicott's body in San Francisco might have applied a white lead cosmetic to his face to improve its appearance as was done to President Lincoln for his final trip from Washington to Illinois. Kennicott's own coat and trousers were strong candidates as a source for the lead. At the time of the Civil War, four different processes, Reimann's, Bullard's, Pant's and Cowles, treated wool fabric with lead acetate to make uniforms waterproof as well as moth- and mildew-resistant.

Despite the high lead levels in Kennicott's body, metallic lead as a cause of death was not considered by anyone because lead poisoning results in a lingering, painful death often preceded by coma, conditions inconsistent with the descriptions of Kennicott's last days. Lead-sealed food cans are specifically discounted as a source of poisoning because everyone on the expedition ate food from the same type of cans, yet Kennicott was the only Western Union man to die in Russian America.

Research prompted the conclusion that, because lead was used so routinely at the time, it isn't possible to determine the source of the excessive levels of lead in Kennicott's body.

Two forms of arsenic were found in Kennicott's remains: methylated, meaning it was part of his body during life, and unmethylated.

Because it is a strong poison, arsenic had multiple and widely diverse uses in the 1800s. Arsenic was a mainstay of medicine, often referred to as "the medical mule." The most popular form of arsenic was Fowler's Solution (potassium arsenate) swallowed for a variety of systemic illnesses. Arsenical paste, made of arsenious acid, sulphate of morphia, and sufficient creosote to form a paste, was recommended for tooth aches due to cavities. Kennicott had many fillings in his teeth and two large, active cavities at his death; he also had two of the paste ingredients available at Nulato. Arsenic was suggested as medicine "in consequence of feebleness of the heart," so Kennicott may have used this remedy after his fainting episode in San Francisco. All of these uses would result in methylated arsenic.

More probably, the methylated arsenic in Kennicott's remains was absorbed over many years as he prepared specimens for museums since the Smithsonian recommended liberally dusting furred and feathered specimens with arsenic to kill insects. Every collector used it. Bischoff was left at a Sitka hospital because his hands were blistered, probably by arsenic; Bannister at St. Michael's reported poisoning his fingers with it. The small amount (1.18 microgram per gram) of metabolized arsenic in Kennicott's remains would not have killed him.

Larger amounts of unmethylated arsenic were found in his hair (24.0 micrograms per gram) and his nails (4.8 micrograms per gram) because the high sulfur content of hair and nail bind arsenic once the arsenic is made soluble by water. Why was arsenic in his coffin?

When Kennicott left St. Michael's for Unalacleet at the end of September 1865, he withdrew twenty pounds of arsenic from the scientific supplies left in charge of Bannister, who recorded the transaction. Even though Kennicott had abandoned plans to collect natural history specimens himself, he still encouraged others to collect, as the items on the list suggest. There's no record of what he did with those scientific supplies, but it's possible that he took some of them, including arsenic, to Nulato.

Arsenic was the main ingredient in the embalming fluids used during the Civil War because it effectively reduced the microorganisms responsible for decomposition. In the twentieth century, arsenic was widely used as a desiccant on cotton plants before mechanically harvesting the crop. The men at Nulato may not have known about embalming fluid and the drying effect on plants, but Pease certainly knew how to use arsenic as an insecticide and may have sprinkled it, as liberally as recommended, on Kennicott's body in the days before the coffin was ready.

(See page 143 for complete list of the scientific supplies.)

Nulato
May 1866

Success was assured. Cotter and Dyer found a path through the mountains from the coast; geese and game returned making provisions plentiful; the boats were ready to go up and down the Yukon. But Kennicott was not feeling well. For days he had complained to Pease of dizziness and a strange sensation in his head. Also, he was not sleeping well. Everyone lost sleep because the ice breaking up on the Yukon sounded like the whole world cracking apart and the released bergs ground loudly into each other. Still, the men reported Kennicott was quieter than usual during those days in early May; not sad, exactly, but certainly grave, serious. Perhaps just knowing that his men were speaking against him and had obviously not fully understood his decisions worried him.

To explain himself to his superiors and to his men, Kennicott carefully wrote out the various obstacles he had met and his attempts to overcome them, reasserting his commitment to the telegraph expedition. Reportedly, Kennicott confessed that this section of the Yukon was very much different from the area he had been in before. Neither the country, nor the natives, nor the game were what he had expected. He added that his ignorance had caused him to overpromise what could be accomplished, especially in winter, and he apologized for the difficult situation he had caused the men to face.[1]

Since they were waiting for the river ice to completely break up, Kennicott also considered the future of the river expeditions. "In case of any accident happening to me" he wrote, Ketchum was to take charge of the expeditions from Nulato, making all of the decisions. This letter, establishing a firm chain of command to prevent squabbles in any emergency, would be expected from any group's leader. Still, the many months of exploration around Nulato had presented innumerable chances for deadly accidents; only now did Kennicott formally name a replacement.

Then, Kennicott reportedly felt better and on the evening of

May 12, 1866, was exercising in the fort yard, doing jumping jacks, it was said. Inside their room that night, Kennicott stood beside Adams who was writing in his diary, then said he was tired and would turn in. Adams, looking at Kennicott, "thought he was asleep and I said to myself that is good he will forget his troubles for a time at least, he has been a good deal troubled about the way things have gone since we were landed at St. Michael's and seems to take to heart our many disappoints and failures which though it has been impossible to remedy has taken a severe hold on him and seems to have entirely broken him down...."[2] About two or three in the morning, Kennicott got up, remarking that he could not sleep, and began writing. After writing for a few minutes, he lit his pipe, went outside into the silent fort yard and walked there for a while. Speaking Russian, he greeted the watchman who then opened the gate for him. Since others were obviously awake in the sunlit night to report what Kennicott had done, being awake at three in the morning was not unusual.

The men were not worried when Kennicott did not show up for their usual eight o'clock breakfast, but when he still was not back an hour later they decided to look for him. Knowing he could not go far, Pease and Lebarge strolled down to the river's beach and walked south along the Yukon.[3] Their view down the beach, ordinarily unimpeded, was blocked by six-foot-high bergs recently tossed up by the surging river as it broke its frozen layers. They finally saw Kennicott, about five hundred yards from the fort, stretched out on his back on the beach. He looked peacefully asleep, with both hands on his chest, his black felt broad-brimmed hat tipped slightly over his forehead. There was no sign of a struggle. In fact, scratched into the soil by his side was a rectangle with lines representing the compass points and in the center was Kennicott's compass in its open container, the cover lying a little to one side. He had been working until his last minutes.

Robert Kennicott died on May 13, 1866, almost a year after his pulseless faint in San Francisco on May 17, 1865.

His stunned men carried his body up the river bank and into the fort commander's house where they decided what to do. Not just what they should do, but what should be done with Kennicott's body. None of them could bear to think of leaving Kennicott at Nulato, the site of so much anguish and hardship. Moreover, their work there was done. The overland passage through the moun-

Top: Page from Adams's diary showing the drawing Kennicott made in the shore just before he died.
Bottom: Enlarged, the words are: "Compass lying in the center. Cover a little on one side."

tains for Western Union had been mapped and traversed. There was little reason for them to stay at the fort without the leader who could converse with and had the trust of the natives and who could translate the physical scene into careful survey notations. Besides, they had found the letters from Kennicott on the table in their room. His written plans called for Ketchum, Lebarge, and Lukine to go up river to Fort Yukon in the three-holed baidarka and the rest to go down river to St. Michael's in the open baidara. In the end, the men saw no reason to change those plans. They decided to take the major's body with them to St. Michael's where they hoped Bulkley would permit Pease to take Kennicott home to his family in Illinois. Not that their plan would be easy; a lot could go wrong; but they would try.

With that decision made, and perhaps reflecting their esteem for Kennicott, they followed custom as if they were back home. They ordered a coffin built and, in the meantime, Ketchum and Pease carefully laid Kennicott out. Kennicott could have been buried in whatever he was wearing when he walked out of the fort that morning, or even simply enshrouded. Yet, his men dressed Kennicott formally in his uniform, bound his jaw, tied his legs together, and arranged his arms on his abdomen. Then, covered with an American flag, his body lay in the fort for the traditional three days. Smith and Adams sat with the body the first night and, doubtless, others took their turns.

Interior of Fort Nulato showing the Yukon River in the distance.

The coffin took two days for Lukine and others to construct. The Russian commander contributed boards removed from the partition that separated his rooms from the common barracks; Adams carefully caulked the coffin's seams inside and out with pitch or creosote before it was lined with green baize. On the third day, Kennicott's body was lowered into the coffin and the lid attached. They wrapped what must have been a large, sticky box in one of their waterproof rubber blankets, then buried the coffin as deeply as they could in the permafrost near the grave of a previous fort commander and the grave of Lt. Bernard who searched for Sir John Franklin.

While they waited for the river ice to clear enough for relative safety, they packed their belongings, collected food supplies, and generally prepared for two river expeditions. The group going upstream, against the swollen river's current, would have the harder time. But the downstream group would hardly have it easy. The Yukon, at spring flood, carries not only the usual debris, but also large blocks of ice and long trees, torn from the banks by the water's force. Between those obstacles and the men would be the thickness of sealskin.

Even though the river opened enough for passage, thick ice cakes constantly collided and crashed, adding to the roar of the river itself. In that din and danger, about ten in the morning of May 25, 1866, with salvos of artillery, dipping flags, and the other ceremonies of leave-taking, both expeditions left Fort Nulato. Cotter had gone days earlier to retrace the path through the mountains

The type of open, sealskin boat with a central mast used to take Kennicott's casket and his men down the ice-filled river to St. Michael's.

to Unalacleet. Ketchum, Lebarge, and Lukine went upstream to Fort Yukon; Pease, Adams, Smith, and Dyer went downstream to St. Michael's with Kennicott's body.

Kennicott's coffin was unearthed ten days after burial and thirteen days after death, making everyone worry about their plan. To Smith's relief, "on taking the body up we placed it in the bow and were astonished to find that the coffin made by Lukeen was airtight; that relieved us a great deal for we had feared that the corpse would be so offensive that we would be obliged to leave it."[4] As they raced toward St. Michael's along with the ice floes, the men complained of the hot sun and the swarms of large mosquitoes that fed on them whenever they landed. Still, the dangerous and physically exhausting river trip was otherwise uneventful and sometimes even cheerful, when they stopped at native villages to trade and talk. Now that birds had returned and were nesting, they ate well on roasted meat and cooked eggs. With daylight approaching twenty-two hours a day, the men could sail, or paddle, or ride with the current as long as they liked.

In fifteen days they were at St. Michael's, having traversed five hundred miles of the Yukon and eighty miles of the coastal ocean

from which the ice had melted only recently. Ennis and Bendeleben were waiting for them, having learned the awful news of Kennicott's death from Dyer who left the boat twelve days earlier to go overland to Unalacleet. That same day, June 9, 1866, they placed Kennicott's coffin in a free-standing turret outside of the fort. "A house," said Smith, "devoted to that purpose....About 12 we all went down to the vault when Mr. Bendeleben read the funeral service over the Major."[5]

A souvenir postcard showing a free-standing turret at St. Michael's; perhaps the one in which Kennicott was buried for three months.

A vault or grave in the permafrost inside the turret would protect Kennicott's body from the strong summer sunlight.[6]

Now all they had to do was wait for the ship bringing Bulkley who would reassign them or allow them to go home. Dyer had gone overland to be sure the once-a-year-ship did not leave before the river-running group could reach St. Michael's. Pease wanted to take Kennicott's body to Illinois, Bannister wanted to leave because his face was too tender to take another cold winter. Smith and Adams would stay, putting themselves under Ennis, who now took command of all the Yukon expedition men.

Even though their trip from San Francisco last year had not brought them to St. Michael's until September, they expected this year's supply ship by the end of June. Compared to the activity of exploring at Nulato, there was nothing to do at St. Michael's. Bannister had been complaining of boredom for months. Day after day he recorded, "Nothing of interest happened." Now Smith also complained: "Nothing of any interest has occurred today. No amusement, no excitement of any kind in fact — nothing but eating, smoking, playing cribbage [a card game], sleeping and wait, wait, wait. The fifteen days which may elapse before the ship reaches here will seem as many months."[7] Even the springtime flowers covering the island did not spark their interest. Bannister and Pease managed to vary some days by hunting birds for their natural history collections, but waiting was their main occupation.

On July 11, 1866, Ketchum, Lebarge, and Lukine reached St. Michael's from Fort Yukon, a downstream trip that had covered the thousand river miles in only nineteen days. The firsthand experience of Westerners confirmed what Kennicott had believed from the natives: the Kwichpak on Russian maps and the Yukon on British maps were the same river that empties into the Bering Sea just below Norton Sound. Then, the men relayed something Kennicott would never have believed: no one from the Fraser River group had made it to Fort Yukon. What the St. Michael's men could not know was that the Fraser River party had not completed their assignment. The workmen were sent home in early October 1865 because winter conditions would make their work too difficult. Pope and Rothrock, who continued to explore for a telegraph path, would have died that harsh winter had their native Cree guide not kept them moving when they wanted to sleep and gone for help to rescue the exhausted, emaciated men. Although the Fraser River group never reached Fort Yukon, they did clear a path, set poles, and string hundreds of miles of cable in British Columbia.[8]

On that same July 11, 1866, the Western Union flagship *Nightingale* left San Francisco for her port-to-port voyage, almost a month after the men at St. Michael's began eagerly searching the horizon. Aboard ship, Dall constantly defended Kennicott to keep Bulkley from dismissing him. One of Kennicott's chief detractors was Stephen Field, nephew of Cyrus Field of the Atlantic Telegraph, who wanted desperately to best his uncle at connecting Europe and America.

While anchored at Plover Bay, Siberia, Dall sent a long letter to Baird on September 18, 1866, elaborating some of the politics of the expedition: "Col. B. [Bulkley] has been completely under the control of a parcel of swindling sots and toadies whose advice he has followed to the detriment of the objects of the Company. They have been already at work since we left San Francisco to annoy, obstruct, and even oust all the honest hard workers in the service. On Scammon & the Sci. Corps they have centered a great deal of their venom, and it will shortly be decided at St. Michael where a grand fight is going to come off. I think Rob. [Kennicott] would come down anyhow, but they intend to make him whether or no. I have been fighting them all the summer and have had a bitter and hard time of it for I have not had one friend in whom I could trust implicitly."[9] He maintained that he constantly wrote the company directors, "to deny that the Scientific Corps was a set of fellows who did nothing but catch bugs in brass buttons on high salaries."[10] Dall, who passionately believed in the value of the Scientific Corps, predicted that their scientific results "will keep their [WUTC] memory green when some cheaper and faster method of communication has supplanted the telegraph."[11]

On July 26, 1866, fifteen days after the *Nightingale* sailed out of San Francisco and out of contact, Cyrus Field's underwater transatlantic cable worked. In September 1866, the previous year's failed cable was found, hauled up, and repaired. As the Western Union ships carried supplies and encouragement to their Arctic workers, two of the competitor's telegraph lines carried messages between Europe and America.

A Newsworthy Death
2003

When Cyrus Field's transatlantic cable succeeded, Kennicott's mother must have hoped for his speedy return home. Instead, Mary Kennicott learned of her noted son's death—by reading the local paper.

The Chicago newspaper could publish the shocking information so quickly only because of the telegraph. The story originally appeared in San Francisco papers and then was telegraphed to papers nationwide. The irony could not have been lost on Robert's mother.

Robert had been gone for eighteen months. He was so far away she'd stopped writing, knowing the letters couldn't get to him. Now he was dead. The casual, offhand way the news was stated must have seemed almost cruel.

Eleven lines were printed in the middle of the front page of the *Chicago Tribune* on October 8, 1866 within a group of stories under a general heading: FROM THE PACIFIC COAST. After a sentence about Hawaiian Queen Emma, the paper reported:

> A letter from the Western Union Extension Telegraph party dated St. Michael's Northwest Coast, Aug. 20, says: 'The ships from San Francisco have not yet arrived, but they are expected daily. The telegraph employees have had no direct news from the outer world for more than a year. Col. Kennicott, the leader of the St. Michael's party, died suddenly at Milato Bay last May. The remainder of the party are well. Stores are plenty, and Russian officers have treated the party with great kindness and hospitality.[1]

Two months earlier, in late August 1866, a Russian ship stopped at St. Michael's on her way to Sitka. Adams and Pease both took the opportunity to write their families about Kennicott's death. Adams's letter, going only to San Francisco, reached its destination first. Adams's father took the startling information to the San Francisco papers where it was reported in the *Daily Alta California* on October 4 and in the San Francisco *Bulletin* on October 3. The *Alta* misspelled Kennicott's name but gave the death place correctly. The *Bulletin* spelled Kennicott's name correctly but gave him the wrong rank. Then, someone misread the handwritten "Nu" as "Mi" and added Bay. The *Bulletin's* story was sent by telegraph to the *Tribune*.

Chicago Academy board president Walker telegraphed Baird asking for more information. They knew the Russian American coastline had been accurately mapped, in part by William Stimpson who took over the Academy in Kennicott's absence, but they couldn't find Milato Bay. Mrs. Kennicott not only didn't know why her son died, she couldn't even find the place of his death. Walker wrote Baird: "Mrs. Kennicott is almost killed by the news....It is the saddest thing that could have happened for all at The Grove. The weary waiting of months has terminated as I had feared it might but no one can tell how poor Mrs. Kennicott will ever live through it."[2]

A long article in tribute to Kennicott, in the *Chicago Tribune* on October 9, related his achievements in natural science and ended, "where known he was highly esteemed, not only for his attainments, but for the genial qualities and noble sentiments which marked his heart as being in the right place. His death will be widely regretted."[3] Mary Kennicott still held hope for her son's return. Walker wrote Baird on October 22, "I was out to the Grove yesterday and found Mrs. K quite feeble and broken down. She cannot yet give Bob up as dead and will not until she knows exactly when and how he died."[4]

On October 25, extracts from Pease's letter to his family in Ohio, describing Kennicott's death, the trip down the Yukon, and Kennicott's burial at St. Michael's, were printed in the *Cleveland Daily Herald*. The letter was telegraphed to the *Chicago Tribune* and printed in a more-shortened form on October 27, 1866.[5] Mrs. Kennicott finally had the information she wanted.

Now, all Mrs. Kennicott could do was hope that Robert's body would come home from Russian America.

[For Pease's letter, see page 139.]

Fall-Winter
1866-67

"We have almost given up the vessels coming this year, they are so late. Something must have happened, perhaps shipwreck. They may possibly come yet; the sea will probably be open till the later part of October. I am trying to reconcile myself to the situation as it appears, a rather difficult thing to do."[1]

At St. Michael's, Bannister's diary entry on September 9, 1866, acknowledged his despair. With winter coming and his healing face still tender, he really did not want to stay another whole year in the Far North. Other men were just as anxious. They walked to the island's small hilltop almost daily, straining their eyes for a sail. They clung to rumors of ship sightings until it was obvious they were not true. They checked out pieces of wooden wreckage hoping none were from Western Union vessels. For all they knew, the *Shenandoah*, which finally surrendered to the British in November 1865, was still out there sinking ships.

Just a week later Bannister crowed, "Goodbye to the blues, the *Wright* arrived in the evening...."[2] and ten days after that, on September 25, 1866, the *Wright* towed in to the fort the *Nightingale*, bringing Frederick Whymper and William Dall to receive the news of Kennicott's death.

Dall was devastated. "The rosy clouds which illumined a prospective winter have faded away. The spur, which nerved me to face any danger, and look carelessly on difficulties and trials, by the side of one I loved and trusted, is taken away."[3] He was bereft. "I write in great sorrow. The man who trusted me, loved me, believed in me and whom I loved better than anybody else in the great world is dead!"[4] Dall wrote a very formal pledge to Baird, whom he did not know well, "to continue the work...[of] the late beloved Robert Kennicott of making collections in Natural History in the Arctic..."[5]

When the *Nightingale* left St. Michaels at noon on October 1,

1866, Dall was the only one to note that it carried the body of Robert Kennicott; neither Bannister nor Adams nor Smith records the event. Bannister and Pease also boarded the *Nightingale* which, as flagship of the line, would not go directly to San Francisco but continue her rounds to the other ports. Two days after she left St. Michael's, the outside world learned of Kennicott's death. Bannister finally wrote Baird from Plover Bay, Siberia, adding the plans for Kennicott's body, "His remains are now on board, and Mr. Pease is going through to The Grove with them."[6] On October 15, as the *Nightingale* left Plover Bay, the California Academy of Natural Sciences passed a resolution offering condolences to Kennicott's family and friends. Before the *Nightingale* reached her next port of Petropavlovsk, Kamchatka, Russia, the *Cleveland Daily Herald* printed Pease's letter describing in detail Kennicott's death and the journey with the coffin down the Yukon to St. Michael's.[7]

By the first of November, family, friends, and the scientific communities of San Francisco (where Dall had worked throughout the winter), Cleveland (the home of Pease and Kirtland), and Washington (where Baird had received copies of the articles) all knew of Kennicott's death and had read about the wooden coffin constructed in the Yukon fort of Nulato. The officers and board of Western Union in New York also knew the details because Baird sent them copies of the Chicago newspaper article.[8]

The Chicago Academy of Sciences chose to honor Kennicott by lengthy addresses at its regular meeting on November 13, 1866, which was also Kennicott's birthday. Walker told that friends who were waiting for Kennicott in Fort Yukon wrote in July that he had not come. Then "the bitter sadness of those few lines [printed in the papers] flashed across the continent....It does seem very hard that he should have died so far from home, and without the kind care and attentions a loving friend would have given him....He died alone....He went out in the morning only a little way from the Fort — sat down on the river bank and died. Can anything be sadder?"[9]

Almost a month later, Kennicott's body and the two Scientific Corps members returned to San Francisco. The *Daily Alta California* reported on December 9, 1866, the arrival of the *Nightingale* "at 8 o'clock last night....The *Nightingale* brings about twenty passengers, whose names will be found below, and the remains of the late Major R. Kennicott, en route for Chicago." Among the list of passengers are H. B. Bannister and Chas. Place. [Henry M. Bannister,

Charles Pease.][10]

At this point, Bannister and Pease must have received confirmation of the news they heard before leaving St. Michael's: Cyrus Field successfully laid a transatlantic cable. Western Union's effort was labeled a failure in newspapers just as the two boarded the ship to come home. While the company had not yet formally decided to wrap up operations in Russian America, both men were released from service.

Knowing that Pease intended to bring Kennicott's body to The Grove for burial, everyone had time to plan for a fitting ceremony. Someone, or some group, arranged for Kennicott's body to be transferred from the wooden coffin made in Alaska to the metal one buried in Illinois. No one in Chicago wrote of being surprised to see a metal coffin arrive. In fact, Stimpson wrote Baird, "We found that everything possible had been done; an air-tight metallic coffin prevented any perceptible decomposition...."[11]

Because of the burgeoning telegraph correspondence over Western Union's coast-to-coast wires, instructions for the treatment of Kennicott's body could have been waiting for Pease when he stepped off the *Nightingale*. Pease certainly used the medium: "A telegraphic dispatch was received in this city on Wednesday, from Charles Pease, Jr. stating that he had arrived at San Francisco, with the remains of the late Major Kennicott, and would leave shortly for the East." [12]

But Pease did not "leave shortly." Perhaps part of the reason for his delay was that there was one more member of the Scientific Corps to arrive. Ferdinand Bischoff did not return from Russian America with Bannister and Pease because the *Nightingale* did not call at Sitka, where he spent the year making extensive collections in natural history. Bischoff arrived on December 12, 1866, with thirty-one boxes, "an immense amount of all kinds of specimens,"[13] to add to the two boxes of specimens packed at St. Michael's. This collection merited notice in the *New York Times:* "The Russian American Telegraph Company's steamer *George Wright...* brings a collection of thirty boxes of animal, vegetable and other curiosities from Russian America for the Smithsonian Institute."[14] Bannister and Bischoff repacked the specimens from December 19 to 24 and had "27 boxes and a barrel to go to the S. I."[15]

In the meantime, Pease took a room at the American Exchange hotel while Bannister, who had no money, stayed aboard the ship.

Bannister reports meeting Pease for a walk on December 18, 1866, but does not report what was said or what Pease did in the days between their arrival and departure. He makes no mention of what was done with Kennicott's body during that time. A local newspaper reported, "The remains of Major Kennicott have been carefully preserved, and will be sent with an escort at the expense of the Company, to his friends at Chicago."[16] While Kennicott's remains were sent at Western Union's expense, the fares for Bannister and Pease were deducted from the wages they received the day before they left San Francisco.

They would return home the same way they left: a ship from San Francisco, a trip across the isthmus, a second ship to New York, and then a train to Chicago. Steamship lines maintained regular schedules and could be counted on to arrive on time at the end of the twenty-three-day journey. Several train lines left New York for Chicago on convenient daily schedules.

The *Daily Alta California* reported on Saturday, December 29, 1866, that "The P.M.S.S. Co.'s steamship *Golden Age* leaves for Panama this morning, at the usual hour, with the following cabin passengers: F. M. Bannister, F. Bichoff, Chas. Pease...."[17] Bannister's souvenir card showing the latitude and longitude of Cost Rica and signed by Captain Lapidge on January 10 proves the group celebrated the New Year aboard the *Golden Age*.

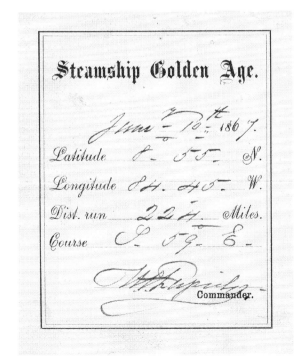

Bannister's souvenir card from the trip to Panama from San Francisco.

Even crossing the isthmus posed no problem this time. Bannister records, "just before sunrise — about 5 A — left ship in Panama directly to train cars but waited 2 hrs before starting. Arrived at Aspinwall about 12 pm....After waiting about an hour we went aboard of our ship the *New York* and left the harbor at about 2 pm."[18] The complete trip was arranged through one ticket, a significant improvement over their tedious and exhausting crossing the previous year. Bannister, Bischoff, and Pease arrived in New York on Sunday afternoon, January 20, 1867, in the middle of a severe snowstorm that effectively shut down the East Coast.

Train schedules show that, on any day after landing in New York, Pease could have taken a fast train directly to Chicago. Instead, he took a train to Cleveland, his hometown. At some point, Pease learned that a child of his had died while he was gone and that his wife was seriously ill. From the Chicago Academy, Stimpson wrote to Baird on January 25, 1867, "Pease telegraphs that he cannot come on account of the sickness of his wife, but sends them [Robert's remains] on by express."[19] A Lake Shore & Michigan Southern express train left Cleveland at five in the morning, arriving in Chicago at seven-thirty in the evening. Stimpson's letter of January 30, 1867, explains that "The remains of poor Robert arrived here [Chicago] on Friday evening last."[20]

After shepherding the body of his childhood friend from Fort Nulato, Russian America, five hundred miles down the ice-filled Yukon River, to San Francisco via Siberia and Kamchatka, down the lengths of both the West and East coasts, across the isthmus, and half across the nation, Pease sent the casket the remaining fourteen hours to Chicago by itself. He did not attend Kennicott's funeral. As the Cleveland newspaper remarked, "The devotion shown by his [Kennicott's] early playmate and friend, Lieut. Pease, in so carefully guarding his remains through all the desolate region he was obliged to travel, with no friend to receive him in his self-imposed offices, is deserving of the highest commendation."[21]

Before Pease left New York for Cleveland, Bannister left New York for Washington. He talked with Baird for an hour or so at the Smithsonian on January 22 and then caught the evening train for Chicago. He attended the funeral of his mentor even though a snowstorm on January 26 covered the country from St. Louis to Milwaukee.

Two hundred sixty-one days after his death, Robert Kennicott was buried "by the side of his father" at The Grove on Monday, January 28, 1867, in a simple graveside ceremony led by Reverend Robert Collyer, a prominent Chicago minister. Stimpson gives further details: "The burial case was tastefully decorated by [Kennicott's] sisters with white flowers and autumn leaves, and the grave lined with evergreens. There were some singular evidences which made us think that nature sympathized with us in our sad-

William Stimpson, 1860. He continued as Director of the Chicago Academy of Sciences until his death in 1872.

111

ness. As soon as Bob's remains arrived at the Grove on Saturday afternoon, the trees became filled with black-cap titmouse — they stayed until after the ceremony. At the moment when we lowered the body into the grave a covey of quails sitting nearby gave forth their sweet song — not the cheerful "Bob White" of springtime, but the plaintive note by which the scattered covey expressed their anxiety or call each other to the evening rest. It did indeed seem as if the birds that Bob had loved so well were mourning his decease, or had come to watch over his grave, to prevent his being lonely."[22]

Stimpson's description of nature's sympathy was only fitting for Kennicott, the scientist who "named five new species of mammals as well as 33 new species of snakes and two new genera of snakes. He wrote technical descriptions of 40 other species of snakes.... He collected more than a hundred kinds of previously unknown insects and other forms of life that were described as new species by other zoologists. At least 16 species have been named in his honor."[23] Three specimens that he named as new species have been given common names that incorporate his: Kennicott's ground squirrels.

Kennicott grave site at The Grove with the schoolhouse in the background.

Two months later, Stimpson wrote Dall, "I do not know when the death of so young a Scientific man has created so profound a sensation of sorrow, not only in his own city, but throughout the entire country wherever Scientific circles exist."[24] Smithsonian Secretary Henry wrote, "In this dispensation of Providence, science has lost an ardent and successful votary, and the Institution one of its most valued collaborators."[25]

"Maj. Robert Kennicott, one of the greatest explorers and naturalists in the annals of Northwest America....laid his life down, like the brave soldier, at the utmost frontier of the battle fields of Nature." [26]

"...that genius of early Illinois, Robert Kennicott,...perished upon the banks of the Yukon River in Alaska, a martyr to scientific discovery and research..."[27]

"This remarkable, intelligent, sensitive and devoted young scientist...[Robert Kennicott] was in a way sacrificed to the pecuniary busyness of the nineteenth century."[28]

Mercury
2001

After Kennicott's death, Dall assumed the duties of director of the Scientific Corps in Russian America. Since he was no longer acting medical director, he turned in the medical supplies he'd been given. On that supply list at St. Michael's was two ounces of Blue Mass. Something about that didn't seem right.

Not that he shouldn't have had Blue Mass. Nearly everyone used the little blue pill in the 1800s for various reasons. In 1828 the pill was used to cure dysentery; by 1861 it was a staple in the medical chests of Civil War doctors. Dall used it himself on the trip through the isthmus and on shipboard to prevent sea sickness, making it no surprise to find mercury in Kennicott's remains, too. Kennicott had 7.35 micrograms per gram of mercury in his hair; only 1.67 micrograms per gram in his bone. Of those amounts, about 0.025 micrograms per gram was methylated mercury, meaning it was incorporated into his body's tissues during life. Because mercury is now known to damage the central nervous system, the autopsy scientists wanted to know how much Kennicott might have absorbed, as well as how long he'd been exposed.

There was so little mercury in Kennicott's remains it could easily be dismissed as the result of sending specimens to the Smithsonian since both Baird and Henry recommended using mercuric chloride as a substitute for arsenic when preserving mammal skins. Mercuric chloride, also called corrosive sublimate, goes from a solid to a vapor at normal room temperatures. In addition to handling the metal, Kennicott may have inhaled mercury vapors. A list of scientific supplies signed by Dall when he took over from Kennicott contains "2 lbs. Corrosive Sublimate." Chances are both men used it.

Everyone knew mercury was poisonous; that's why they used it. Mercurochrome on a wound killed bacteria and promoted healing. Mercuric chloride disinfected hospitals and killed insects. As calomel, mercuric chloride was rubbed on gums for a teething powder or for a toothache. The blue pill was swallowed as a diuretic, as a laxative, to cure syphilis, and to aid childbirth.

Blue Mass was so accepted at the time that these few sentences were printed as a filler article, without further explanation, in the October 3, 1866, edition of the *Chicago Tribune*: "The *New York Herald* calls the Pittsburgh Convention the 'Blue Mass.' It will undoubtedly put the Nation's liver in good condition, and will clean out all such impurities as Copperheadism." Common knowledge said the elemental grey, shiny metal attached itself to the causes of illness, then passed unabsorbed through the body and was excreted.

Blue Mass (pilulae hydrargyri) was prepared by pharmacists whose individual recipes for the prescription may have varied, but each pill always contained elemental mercury mixed with powdered licorice, rose leaves, honey, and chalk. In addition to reputedly clearing bile from the liver, Blue Mass was the primary prescription for a condition Kennicott complained of since he was twenty: melancholy. In the summer of 1857, when he worked in southern Illinois, he wrote home repeatedly about feeling "low, miserably defeated and sorrowful without cause." In winter 1862, when collecting through British America, Kennicott wrote of a "hibernation of the intellect," a "stopper on mental exertion." By 1865, on the way to San Francisco, he wrote he'd "become semi-comatose" soon after starting and "fell into one of my habitual semi-comatose states" on the way to the Yukon. In the Yukon in 1866 he wrote he was "in a state of profound coma lately out of which I only awaken to become low spirited enough to cut my throat…"

Much earlier, at age twenty-one, he debated taking Blue Mass, and at twenty-eight, he wrote "…only blue mass…can keep me from being discouraged." There is no direct statement that Kennicott took Blue Mass, only the circumstantial evidence of those letters. If he took it, did Blue Mass cause neurological damage?

Until recently, the answer would have been no because the mercury was still assumed to pass through the digestive system unabsorbed. Then, scientists curious about aspects of Abraham Lincoln's life did some research.

Lincoln, president in Kennicott's time, was known to take Blue Mass but stopped because he thought it contributed to his ill tempers. In 2001, Dr. Norman Hirschhorn and Dr. Ian Graves, both of the University of Minnesota, and Dr. Robert Feldman at Boston University School of Medicine analyzed evidence that Lincoln's demeanor was affected by the Blue Mass he took for melancholy. They reconstructed the blue pill and determined that "dispersing the mercury into fine particles and increasing its surface area was meant to assure its absorption into the body….The solid element of mercury absorbed from two pills would have been 750 micrograms. The EPA indicates that only up to 21 micrograms of any form of mercury per day may be safely ingested."[1] The "reconstructed 'blue pill' was a round, gray pellet the size of a peppercorn. If taken at the normally prescribed dose of the time — one pill two or three times a day — it would deliver nearly 9,000 times the amount of mercury that is deemed safe for people by current health standards."[2] "Someone who ate these little pills would have seriously risked poisoning, absorbing both vapor and solid element."[3]

Depending on the condition it was prescribed to cure, the amount of mercury per pill varied. In Ellingwood's *American Materia Medica of 1919*, the recommended dose was from ¼ of a grain to 5 grains. During the Civil War, a cathartic prescription was from 5 to 15 grains. (15 grains equals 1 gram) The Army's Standard Supply Table allocated a Civil War regiment, about eight hundred men, eight 8-ounce bottles of the blue pills. The two ounces Dall left at St. Michael's probably was an appropriate amount for the thirty men working there.

Two other lists of Western Union medical supplies exist; neither includes Blue Mass. When Dall received medical supplies from Dr. Fisher at St. Michael's on September 27, 1866, there was no Blue Mass on the list. When Dall turned over the same medical supplies to F. M. Smith at Unalacleet on October 25, 1866, the list contained two ounces of Blue Mass.

As acting medical director, Dall may have decided Western Union was remiss in not including such a common prescription as Blue Mass and bought the medicine himself, as he did other drugs a year earlier. Or, the medicine could have been his personal supply that he decided was more valuable for the group to have. Yet, it's also possible that Dall was bringing his friend and mentor, Kennicott, a fresh supply of his medication and then left it with the group's supplies. If so, Kennicott may have been taking mercury as Blue Mass, steadily as a preventative or intermittently as needed, for ten years or more.

Still, mercury was not the cause of Kennicott's death. The effects of mercury poisoning are generally chronic, or building over time, rather than acute, or happening suddenly. Kennicott never mentioned at any point the standard symptoms of mercury poisoning such as disturbed vision, or a "pins and needles" sensation in his hands and feet. Nor did his associates comment on any lack of coordination, a common result of neurological damage, which surely would have been apparent in his work with specimens.

It's possible, though, that any neurological damage might have made him cross, have affected his relations with his men, and made it harder for him to deal effectively with the numerous problems he found on the Yukon expedition.

Interpretation

Kennicott's Death 2004

Engraving of Kennicott ordered by Stimpson for use in Transactions.

Over time, various causes have been given for Kennicott's death:

- Disease of the heart in September 1866
- Organic disease of the heart in January 1867
- An electric death in June 2001

But first, in summer 1866, there was silence. A silence so loud it seems orchestrated. No one was willing to answer the first question everyone asks after learning of a death: "How did he die?"

When Adams wrote his family of Kennicott's death, he didn't suggest a cause. The San Francisco newspaper, not wanting to seem negligent when printing his letter, added "No further particulars."

Pease's long letter to his family not only doesn't answer the question, but cribs almost directly from Adams's diary entry on the event: "He had many disappointments and failures since our arrival at St. Michaels, which though it has been impossible to remedy, had taken a severe hold on him, and seemed to have entirely broken him down." That implies a cause but doesn't name one.

Ennis, Kennicott's second-in-command, submitted an official report on June 30, 1866, saying only, "[Kennicott's] death was sudden and his last act on earth was the taking of bearings of the Kvichpak and tributaries."

When the other men wrote letters, Bannister wrote nothing; not to his parents, not to the Chicago Academy, not to the Smithsonian. He didn't even speculate on a cause in his diary.

Were they all just waiting for a doctor to make a medical judgment? Or had they determined a cause of death they were reluctant to share?

Dall finally composed the words that everyone else was thinking. Dall heard the awful circumstances, all the rumors and innuendoes, and wrote from St. Michael's that Kennicott "died last May of disease of the heart on a desolate northern beach, alone!" He wrote his mother, "Dear Robert Kennicott died of heart disease added to by ingratitude and worry..."[1] In another letter, he expands on the cause: "He was murdered; not by the merciful knife but by slow torture of the mind. By ungrateful subordinates, by an egotistical and selfish commander, by anxiety to fulfill his commands."[2] In his official circular to the scientific community, he wrote Kennicott's death was caused by "the heart disease superinduced by excessive anxiety and care in relation to the success of his party and the explorations of which he had charge."[3]

In Dall's Victorian America, certain topics were simply not spoken of or, if they had to be mentioned, were veiled in polite, lofty phrases whose true meanings were commonly understood. Dall used such a coded phrase in his letters describing Kennicott's death. "Disease of the heart" was not a medical diagnosis, yet the people receiving his letters would have understood its meaning because the phrase was commonly used to conceal socially unacceptable causes of death. An 1859 newspaper article reported on the attempted cover-up for a recent death caused by opium, alcohol and other "distasteful causes," explaining that " 'disease of the heart' is the mantle of charity, which the politic coroner and the sympathetic physician throw over the graves of genteel people."[4] Dall may have used a recognizably charitable

phrase that he then elaborated to suggest Kennicott committed suicide. His words and Pease's had the desired effect because Walker of the Chicago Academy concluded, "His disappointments finally killed him."[5]

Dall's official notice, delivered to California's scientists when the *Nightingale* landed in early December 1866, was printed in the local paper, "Major Robert Kennicott, died in May last of disease of the heart."[6] Bannister picked up Dall's refrain when he finally wrote his parents: "I suppose that you have already most of the particulars that he died very suddenly at Nulato the cause being supposed to be disease of the heart."[7]

Yet, on January 1, 1867, after Pease and Bannister returned to San Francisco with Kennicott's body, the expedition's surgeon-in-chief, Dr. Henry Fisher, who was also on the ship, reported officially to Bulkley, "Major R. Kennicott, Chief of the Youkon division...died at Noolato on the Youkon river May 13 1866 from organic disease of the heart."[8]

Pease and Adams, who were at Nulato when Kennicott died, strongly suggested suicide. Dall, who had observed Kennicott's mood swings in San Francisco and thought him "absurdly suspicious of everyone,"[9] evidently agreed with their suggestion. Even Walker, who knew Kennicott from his work in Chicago, could see the possibility. Yet, Dr. Fisher added "organic," implying a natural death caused by a physical heart condition.

What could have happened to change the diagnosis from an implied suicide to a clearly stated natural death?

During the long voyage under sail from St. Michael's to San Francisco, Fisher had many hours in which to talk about Kennicott with both Pease and Bannister. Each of them held clues to Kennicott's death. Pease could have reported Kennicott's complaint, days before his death, of dizziness and a ringing in his head. Fisher would have recognized both as symptoms of a heart's failure to pump blood to the brain. Pease could have detailed the frightening pulseless faint Kennicott had the year before in San Francisco, and Fisher would have seen that as a failure of the heart as well. Bannister could have added the episode of vertigo Kennicott experienced that unnerving January evening in Chicago at the Academy. That makes two strong events of Kennicott's heart failing to pump sufficient blood within a sixteen-month period plus an indication of heart failure in the week before he died.

Kennicott's death position would also have been a clue to Fisher. Everyone agreed that Kennicott was lying on his back with both hands on his chest. A failing heart often causes left-side chest pain that varies from mild to agonizing. To relieve such a pain, Kennicott stretched fully out on the river bank and then may have pressed hard on his left chest.

Fisher could have reasonably concluded that Kennicott died of natural causes: organic heart disease. Kennicott's heart attack was long enough and strong enough, this time, to kill him.

Two and a half years after Kennicott died, when Dall returned from the Yukon in 1868, he wrote Baird, "You doubtless have heard a rumor which I at first believed, with everyone else, that Robert K. committed suicide. I know how glad you will be to know that I have irrefragable [indisputable] proof that he died of valvular disease of the heart, aggravated by mental depression, caused by the villainous conduct of W. H. Ennis, who after his death circulated the above-mentioned lie."[10] Sadly, neither Baird nor Dall records the indisputable proof.

Strangely, Dall did not mention "valvular disease of the heart" when he wrote of Kennicott's death in *Transactions*. He described Kennicott's peaceful appearance and sleeplike position, but did not give a specific cause of death in the published account. Even so, by 1869 everyone agreed that Kennicott died of natural causes.

Unfortunately, the word didn't get back to Adams, who remained in Alaska for several years after all the Western Union men left. In the journal he wrote fifty years later to accompany his diary, he states that Kennicott was buried "in the coffin made in the interior of Russian America."[11] He obviously didn't know about the metal casket just as he didn't know about the organic cause of Kennicott's death.

Since the official reports of Kennicott's naturally caused death are unpublished, and Dall's published account in *Transactions* gave no cause, the public was left with the cause given in Adams's journal. So, a 1972 book could declare, "The brilliant naturalist Robert Kennicott exulted in the freedom of the remote Yukon

Valley. A few months later he killed himself."[12] A 2001 book stated, "There being no final, conclusive word on the matter, it will have to remain an Arctic mystery."[13]

No longer.

The autopsy of Kennicott, a careful reading of the events leading up to the day of his death, and the description of the death scene by several witnesses all lead to the conclusion that Kennicott died an electric death, a fitting description for the death of a man who worked to extend the electric wire of the telegraph and whose company cap was decorated with electric flashes. Medically, an electric death means one in which the heart is beating one second and isn't the next. An instant death. Not one of either gentle decline or of labored breathing. Immediate.

Not, then, a death by strychnine.

Adams wrote that the men all knew Kennicott had swallowed strychnine because foam came out of Kennicott's mouth later on the day he died and because the vial of strychnine he said he had to kill animals couldn't be found. Adams evidently didn't know that strychnine, a powerful stimulant, acts on the central nervous system and in high doses can result in a convulsive death. A toxic dose is commonly followed by a series of bodywide muscle contractions that produce uncontrollable violent movements of the arms and legs. A fatal dose at last causes a rigid arching of the body until only the head and heels touch the ground.

Everything about Kennicott's death scene contradicts that kind of death. All the witnesses agree: He was on his back, as if asleep, his hands on his chest. His compass, carefully in its container, and the container cover were at his side. A drawing he'd made in the beach beside him was so clear that Adams could copy it into his diary margin. Nothing was disturbed; nothing tossed about. No rigid arch.

The foaming at the mouth that Adams observed? The official autopsy report states, "…if the upper part of Kennicott's body was carried in a lower position than the extremities at least part of the time during transport of the body up the embankment and into the fort, gravity would have caused venous blood to flow into the lungs from which, without a beating heart, it could not escape. Such increased pressure within the pulmonary circulation could have been responsible for the extrusion of plasma that subsequently appeared as oral froth."[14]

Kennicott did not commit suicide by swallowing strychnine. He may have been discouraged, but he did not give up. His heart gave out.

Kennicott's Preservation
2010

Even after determining what caused Kennicott's death, there was still one more question: What caused his body to be so well preserved that Stimpson, nine months later, could see no perceptible decomposition as he looked on Kennicott through the casket's glass face plate? Stimpson attributed the preservation to "an air-tight metallic coffin," but he must have known that state-of-the-art metal caskets weren't available in the remote, rustic forts of Russian America where Kennicott died. By the time Kennicott's body could be placed in a metal casket in San Francisco, seven months had passed and decomposition should have been very perceptible. Something must have happened to Kennicott's body in Russian America to preserve it.

Most likely, Kennicott's body was preserved by a combination of the timing of his burial, the coffin he was buried in, and the land he was exploring.

Several hours after he died, Kennicott was brought to the fort and laid out for burial. In the two days it took to construct a coffin, Kennicott's body lay on a plank in the fort. During that time, in the dry cold air, some moisture in the body would have evaporated. Based on the arsenic found in Kennicott's remains, that chemical may have been sprinkled on his body to kill the insects that hasten decay. The drying qualities of arsenic may have helped reduce the body's moisture.

The coffin was built as tightly as possible; then Adams coated the joints of the boards, both inside and out, with creosote to seal it even tighter. Creosote, or pine tar, was listed among the medical supplies at St. Michael's because it was used as an antiseptic, meaning the creosote on the joints would have helped to reduce the bacteria in the coffin. The sticky creosote on the inside was covered with green baize, a tightly woven, soft, wool cloth. The most popular green dye of the time was a compound of arsenic, Paris Green, so it's possible the fabric of the coffin helped reduce insects.

After Kennicott's body was lowered into the box and the lid secured, the whole box was covered with a rubber blanket, to keep moisture out according to Adams. But the blanket—and the creosote—would also have sealed out air. Then Kennicott was buried as deeply as possible, about two feet, in the thawing permafrost.

"The conditions essential to putrefaction are, (1) moisture, (2) a temperature between 32° F and 200° F, (3) atmospheric air, (4) bacteria."[1] With or without intention, the men at Nulato reduced these conditions. As Paul Fledzik, curator of the anatomical collections at the National Museum of Health and Medicine observed, the body's moisture was reduced by being uncoffined for almost three days and then was additionally absorbed by the fabrics and coffin wood.[2] Air transfer was sealed off by the creosote and rubber blanket; creosote killed some bacteria; arsenic killed some insects. In the controlled micro-climate of the coffin, the permafrost kept the body's temperature at or below freezing. Kennicott's body became mummified in the cold, dry conditions.

Thirteen days after Kennicott's temporary, shallow burial, when the men dug up the coffin, Smith noted that there was no aroma of putrefaction. It may be that the creosote and the rubber blanket, used to keep air out, also kept air in. But it's possible that mummification had already begun. Then, the coffin was kept cold at the bottom of a sealskin boat as the men traveled the icy Yukon. At St. Michael's, the coffin was placed in the permafrost within a closed blockhouse that kept the temperature cool.

On the way to San Francisco, the coffin was probably in an unheated hold of the ship. When in the city, it could have been taken to an ice house or to a public vault, both common practices at the time. While in San Francisco, Kennicott's body was transferred to a metal casket in which his already mummified body continued to be preserved so that Stimpson could comment on it in Chicago.

Decoding Bannister
2003

On the day he learned of Robert Kennicott's death, June 2, 1866, Henry Bannister wrote in his diary: "After ten a boat from Unalakhleet arrived bringing Ennis, Bendeleben, & Greene. They bring bad news of the death of Maj. Kennicott. He died very suddenly at Nulato on the 13th of May."

On the next line, Bannister wrote: *"Gsyh muz nip.h nv u.oo az yu ....."*

The first diary entry was published in 1942, along with all the other entries written in English, as part of *The First Scientific Exploration of Russian America and the Purchase of Alaska* by James Alton James. The next lines, as well as fourteen similar entries and the many single words written in code, appear only in Bannister's handwritten diary. The diary itself was discovered in 1939, when James urged Bannister's daughter to search for it, almost seventy-five years after it was written.

As the investigation into Kennicott's death began in 2001, all possibilities were open. No one had a firm idea of why Kennicott died, so any information that could be teased out of the written record was vital. The coded phrases of Bannister, a longtime co-worker and pos-

Diary page showing Bannister's coded passage the day he learned Kennicott died.

sible confidant, might contribute critical information or at least some clues to Kennicott's death. It was essential to break Bannister's code.

A crypographer friend of Owsley's took the initial step by tallying the frequency of the letters used. When she hadn't reported any progress in her painstaking task after a few short months, I impatiently contacted the Museum of Cryptology just outside Washington, DC, hoping that someone there might be tempted to tackle the code. At that time, 2002, every possible person was involved with communications relating to the war in Iraq. Next, I contacted two professors of computer science at the University of Minnesota who agreed to encourage their students to take on Bannister's code as a special project. I never heard from the professors again.

I know very little about codes, but I had learned something about Bannister. He was very scholarly. By age twelve he had learned both Latin and Greek from his father, a professor of Hebrew at the Garrett Biblical Institute attached to Northwestern University. Although Bannister had a high opinion of his abilities, I thought it unlikely that he created his very own code because he seemed more a follow-the-rules type than an invent-the-rules type. But he might, I thought, have prided himself on being an explorer in the mold of Lewis and Clark and might have used the code President Jefferson urged them to use. Since it was relatively simple, I tried it on Bannister's work. All I got was gibberish.

In the meantime, staff members at The Grove combed Bannister's original diaries for any other examples of the code and tried their hands at decoding. They beavered away underground at Northwestern University's Archives but found no more coded passages in any of Bannister's other diaries. In the Smithsonian Archives, I found no examples or mentions of code among Kennicott's friends, the young Smithsonian scientists who might have used a secret code just for the fun of it.

Then, author Dan Brown steamrolled the world with his best-selling novel, *The Da Vinci Code.* Along with a few million others, I devoured the plot; but I also savored the codes. One cipher he described was so simple that I easily comprehended it. He called it a "fold-over code" because the last half of the alphabet folds back, in reverse order, under the first half:

a b c d e f g h i j k l m
z y x w v u t s r q p o n

The word 'man' becomes 'nzm.' The word 'just' becomes 'qfhg.'

This code uses the same process as the *At Bash*, one of the oldest Hebrew cipher systems, which Bannister could have absorbed from his linguist father. Maybe a nice, basic code was all Bannister needed. If the words could be deciphered, they would be read for the first time in one hundred forty years. In true detective-show fashion, late one night by the glow of a single desk lamp, I tried the fold-over code on Bannister's phrases.

It worked.

Or, rather, it worked well enough that I could make out many words. But not all of them. Bannister obviously understood the problems English presents to any cipher. For example, in English the *th* combination is used often, *s* and *ed* appear regularly at the end of words, *e* is the most common letter. The cautious Bannister, with time on his hands, concealed his thoughts by using various ways of encoding the common letters and words. He was also fastidious. He printed very carefully, almost drawing his letters, in dark, unfading ink with no smudges or smears. That was important because Bannister left some letters uncoded, indicating them by microscopic dots under the letter. Then, he used dot combinations in place of letters, almost-stenographic curves for *with, for* and *of*, an apostrophe as *h*, a dash to mean *e,* etc., etc. He obviously intended his words to stay coded, for his eyes only.

Perhaps all Bannister wanted to do was to stimulate his own mind in the depressingly long, dark days of Arctic winter. Using a code would occupy his mind while preventing others at St. Michael's from reading his writing. Bannister doesn't mention sharing his room in the fort, but he most likely did since there were two beds in it. In any case, there was little privacy in the fort. Bannister and two other Western Union men lived in the fort the whole twelve months they spent in Russian America. Pease also spent time there and other men who spoke and read English came and went. The rest of the fort's personnel obviously spoke Russian. So Bannister couldn't write in English, the Americans could read it; he couldn't write in Cyrillic, the Russians could read it. If he wanted to keep something private, he needed a code.

What did he have to say that was so important that no one else could know it?

The first passage I decoded said, "Must try to control my tongue more than I do." Hardly earth shattering, but a revelation nonetheless. Bannister was an only child, named after his minister professor father who taught at Cazenovia seminary in New York before bringing his family to live in the Methodist university town of Evanston, Illinois. Bannister was just twenty when he was at St. Michael's, and a strongly principled young man. He tried very hard to keep the Sabbath and to resist the temptations of alcohol and women. Those preferences might not have made him fun company among the others on the expedition. In fact, he may have been hard to like and easy to hector. Dall called him "incorrigible, the saints couldn't get along with him…" and elaborated, "He is the son of a Methodist minister, and looks just like one; while I bear him no ill wish I must say he is the least obliging and most obstinate fellow I ever saw with any pretensions to Christianity."[1] When Bannister was sent back from the Fraser River party after one month, there were rumors that he had been teased and tormented so much by other men that he pulled a knife on one of them. That sounds a bit impulsive for the tightly-buttoned Bannister, but not implausible. The tormenting continued on the voyage back to the States a full year later, as Bannister recounted in his diary.

Bannister began his diary at the official start of the expedition in New York in March 1865, and kept a daily record of events until the group arrived in San Francisco. The diary stops just before the ship docked and doesn't pick up again until Bannister is with the Fraser River group. The tumultuous, critical days in San Francisco that resulted in the split of the Scientific Corps are condensed into: "My stay in San Francisco was of only three weeks duration but I made the most of that time. Made a short visit to my friends in Santa Clara and had a very pleasant time.... Did not like Frisco very much, was not in a good state of mind to enjoy my stay there. Joined Maj. Pope's party to go to British Columbia and left on the 17th of May for Victoria, Vancouver Isld on the steamer *Sierra Nevada*."[2] After that, his entries are sometimes daily and sometimes condensed into paragraphs covering weeks of time. There are no coded passages from New York all the way to St. Michael's in the Yukon. In December 1865 the diary entries stop entirely until March 1, 1866.

In a New Year's Eve snow storm that winter, Bannister severely froze his face when returning to St. Michael's from Unalacleet and he spent quite a while in bed recovering. He was never able to return to working outdoors in the winter because his face was so painful. But he may not have been completely idle. When the daily entries resume, Bannister gives two dates for the days, using both the Eastern and the Western calendars. He may have become more confident in the Russian language and the Cyrillic alphabet during this time, since he gives the days of the week in Russian and English. Now, for the first time, sentences appear in code.

There are only fifteen separate coded entries between the first one on March 11, 1866, and the last one on November 28, 1866, shortly before he returned to San Francisco. The coded sentences do not relate directly to the uncoded diary entries. In fact, few even relate to the expedition. Most are personal, telling of Bannister's relationships with other men or of his resolves to behave better. Yet, when he learned of Kennicott's death, Bannister took the time to encode, "This news makes me feel as if I had lost one of my best friends in the world. No one is his enemy now! But all own his goodness and worth. Pease is bringing his body here by way of the river."

At the same time as the coded entries appear, Bannister repeats regularly in English, "Nothing of interest occurred." He confines himself to his room or to the fort, only occasionally taking walks when the weather is fine. He reads, plays chess, and works sporadically at his record-keeping. Bannister seems to recognize his depressive lethargy when, on April 14, he writes, "I think that living in this country during the winter as I have been obliged to has a very enervating effect. I want more excitement, have never been so lazy before."[3] Perhaps encoding personal thoughts, no matter how insignificant, was Bannister's way of preventing even further "laziness."

Evidently, Bannister wasn't able to prevent his outspokenness. In his last coded diary entry of November 1866, he was still trying to control his tongue, just as he wrote in his coded entry of the previous April. In the end, Bannister's code helped only a little in answering questions about Kennicott's death. But, it allowed me to recognize that Henry Martyn Bannister was a very young man in a very unusual situation, a situation so unusual that he never again needed the fold-over code in his diaries.

Bannister's Decoded Passages

Sunday, March 11, 1866 (February 28)

Bandy [Bendeleben] seems mad over the chess _____ of yesterday. I hope ___ permanently. Shall try to cons____ him _____ _____ all over.

Friday, March 23 (March 12)

Bhndy [Bendeleben] mad again and will probably stay so this time. I shall try to have none myself.

Tuesday, March 27 (March 16)

Have made up with Bendeleben.

Wednesday, April 4 (March 24)

Evening storming. _____ _____.

Friday, April 20 (April 9)
Three separate entries:

My face worries me most of all with its redness, and I show it a great deal to much. I hope it ____all is off soon. But it is very slow about it, it seems to me. All's right _____, I hope. All's for the best. [Bannister froze his face in the beginning of January.]

Shall try to knock off bad habit from this time forth. May God [in Cyrillic] help me! It is sin of the tongue.

Commence the good practice today, that of cleaning my teeth. Shall do it after each principle meal.

Friday, April 27 (April 16)
Shall ___ Nicolai [an Indian] to make ___ up _____ shot for me. _____ rubles more __ will be.

Saturday, April 28 (April 17)
Did not remember to keep ___ Sabbath today as I had ought to have done.

Must try to keep the Sunday of this place as I would keep my own day at home.

Saturday, June 2 (May 22)

This news makes me feel as if I had lost one of my best friends in the world. No one is his enemy now! But all own his goodness and worth. Pease is bringing his body here by way of the river.

Monday, August 6 (July 26)

___ _light the parka for __ caps. _____ _____ _____ _____.

September 10 (August 30)

Mike [Lebarge], Bandy [Bendeleben], Cotter, Chappel, Dyer, Smith, Adams, Dennison __, and Greene stay here in case the ships do not come! Ennis, Ketchum and Pease start for Kodiak when winter sets in.

Monday, October 15 [aboard ship to US]
__Had a little row with _____ _____ [Russian name]. He proved himself no gentleman, and I shall have no more to do with him.

Thursday, November 1
General Abase with/for Dall _____ turning. Dr. Fisher leading. Has been trying to prejudice Ennis against him. Probably he _____ his _____!!

Wednesday, November 28, 1866

Must try to control my tongue more than I do. May God help me from this time forth.

Kennicott's Strychnine
2008

When Adams determined that Kennicott's death was suicide, he stated that Kennicott carried a vial of strychnine to kill large animals for the Smithsonian; he implied it was common knowledge. How did the men know Kennicott had a small, easily concealed, vial of strychnine with him? Why did Kennicott tell them the strychnine was to kill animals when, months earlier, he'd told Baird he was giving up all chance to collect?

No documents fully answer those questions. Still, it's possible to piece together a plausible set of events.

On Kennicott's earlier trip through British America, the Smithsonian provided large bottles of strychnine; there was no strychnine in the list of supplies for the Scientific Corps in the Yukon. On the earlier trip, Kennicott's family sent him one ounce of strychnine, obviously for his personal use. Very likely, the small vial of strychnine he carried in the Yukon was also for his personal use.

Whether Kennicott swallowed strychnine in medicinal doses throughout his British American trek isn't reported. Nor does anyone record him taking strychnine during the stressful months establishing the Chicago Academy of Sciences. But there was no denying the likelihood of a heart condition when he nearly fainted

in January 1865. There is no report of his fainting when he and others rowed, polled, and dragged rafts of passengers during the isthmus crossing. Yet, when he fell back pulseless in San Francisco in May 1865, revived only by strong spirits, Kennicott must have appreciated that it was a scant four months since he became so dizzy in Chicago.

Kennicott couldn't return to Washington or Chicago, or even stay in San Francisco, without ruining his reputation. If he had a weakly pumping heart, perhaps he could stimulate it with strychnine. Had he been taking it all along for that purpose? (A similar condition, bradycardia, is now treated by implanting a pacemaker.)

According to Dall in *Transactions*, during the unloading of the *Golden Gate* at St. Michael's, a man became drunk on medical alcohol, causing Kennicott to poison it. The Western Union medical supply list doesn't contain alcohol, perhaps because the mission statement of the Western Union Telegraph Company asserts there will be "no intoxicating spirits in camp."[1] But there's a small amount on Bannister's list of medical supplies at St. Michael's, contributed, Dall says, by the ship's captain.

However, Dall's story doesn't mention the scientific alcohol that had to have been unloaded; alcohol was the preferred method for preserving some specimens. Not only had alcohol in corked vials had been given to each of the Western Union ships to encourage the men to collect, but Dall had written Baird complaining bitterly that Bulkley had only provided a meager forty gallons of alcohol in wooden casks that would allow the liquid to evaporate.[2] Some of those casks, quantity unspecified, had been left with Bischoff in Sitka; ten gallons might be a reasonable guesstimate for him to keep. Dall had kept five gallons for his own use on the way back to San Francisco.[3] That means Kennicott may have had twenty-five gallons of preservation alcohol at St. Michael's when he withdrew two gallons as he left for Unalacleet. Compared to the two hundred gallons Dall received the next year for two seasons of work, Kennicott's supply was decidedly scant.[4] The remaining alcohol was too essential to science to chance men drinking it. Probably, the alcohol Kennicott poisoned was the preservation supply.

What did Kennicott have to use as poison? In the scientific supplies, only arsenic might have worked, but was itself intended to preserve specimens. Both arsenic and alcohol had to last until supply ships returned next summer. Would Kennicott have used one critical scientific preservative to save another? More likely, he reached for his own vial of strychnine. Whether he put enough strychnine in each cask to kill a man didn't matter. What counted was that the men believed he had.

Having revealed his strychnine, Kennicott now had to explain why he had it.

Strychnine was so commonly used that the men would have known the many conditions for which it was prescribed. If Kennicott had been taking strychnine for something minor, such as upset stomach, he easily could have said so. He evidently couldn't tell the truth so he chose the fiction, once true, that he had it to kill large animals for the Smithsonian.

If this conjecture is correct, Kennicott would have continued taking the strychnine, on the tip of his penknife, out of view of his men, throughout that trying winter at Nulato. Kennicott's men couldn't find the strychnine vial after his death. Perhaps he lost it or used his last grains just as winter broke, giving him intimations of his own death as his men concluded later. Was that what was making him "serious" as Bannister said? Then Bannister added that Kennicott must have been feeling better just before his death because he was seen doing jumping jacks in the courtyard of the fort. Possibly Bannister misinterpreted. Kennicott may have felt worse, not better, and used physical exertion in place of strychnine to stimulate his heart.

Would Kennicott have lived if his supply of strychnine hadn't run out? Impossible to say. But did he use it to commit suicide? Medically, no, absolutely not. Yet, people commit suicidal acts every day. Adults push children out of the way of cars and are run over themselves. Teenagers go to rescue a friend in deep water and drown. Kennicott saved his scientific work by using his medicine, strychnine. Did he know that could be a suicidal act? Probably, yes.

Kennicott's Casket
2004

Who paid for the very expensive metal casket that allowed Kennicott's face to be viewed by his family one last time?

The casket could have been purchased when Pease, Bischoff, and Bannister arrived in New York. Pease and Kirtland could have bought it in Cleveland. In either of those cities, accomplishing the purchase and the transfer of the body in time to make the required train schedules would have required quick and coordinated action, difficult even with the help of the telegraph. More important, the wood coffin built seven months earlier under the conditions in Nulato might not last the one additional month that the ship-and-rail journey would take. In San Francisco, the men had time to make arrangements but they had little money for an expensive casket. Western Union paid the Scientific Corpsmen only the day before they left for the East, at the end of December 1866.

Various possibilities seemed not to be probable. Western Union could have paid for the casket just as they did for its transport to Chicago, but they took public credit only for the transport. The Kennicott family could have sent money to buy it since it was similar to his father's casket, but there's no record in the family's extensive files of doing that. The Chicago Academy could have bought it; their records burned in the Chicago Fire. If the Smithsonian bought it or contributed to its purchase, the expense isn't recorded in the ledgers. There was no official correspondence from Baird to the Chicago Academy about a casket. There was no letter from Baird to the Kennicott family offering to pay; no thank-you letter from the family. Of course, Baird could have handled payment privately and received a private thank-you.

Still, the casket question lingered. Since the men had the most time and could find many casket stores in San Francisco, who did they know there who had money and who cared enough about Kennicott to want to see him buried in a casket worthy of his reputation?

Then, I learned the answer to my question about the ribbons on Kennicott's sleeves and thought I might have the answer to the casket question as well.

At Kennicott's autopsy, each sleeve of his shirt had a narrow, grosgrain ribbon sewn onto the upper section, approximately level with his heart. The ribbon didn't encircle the sleeve; each end was carefully stitched in place about three-quarters around the loose, blousy sleeve. In addition, before they were stitched down, each ribbon was tied in an open knot, as if it once held something. Herbs? Flowers? Was it likely that the men in Nulato would have placed aromatics on the body? On closer examination, each ribbon was made of two small pieces of ribbon carefully stitched together. The fine stitching was much too time-consuming to have been done when Kennicott was laid out; the ribbons must have been on the sleeve before then. What were those ribbons?

A costume specialist took one look at a picture of the ribbon with its open knot and said, "I've never seen one of those; I've only heard about them. It's a lover's knot."[1]

The custom began with sailors who wanted to know whether the woman they cared for also cared for them. A sailor gave his lady a length of rope tied in an open knot. If she returned the rope without a knot, he knew to look elsewhere for a mate. If she returned it as it was sent, he didn't give up hope but knew he needed to make more effort. If she pulled the knot tight, he could plan a wedding.[2] Kennicott was "wearing his heart on his sleeve" and was "ready to tie the knot."

No one in the Yukon mentions this addition to Kennicott's clothing, nor does anyone mention teasing Kennicott about his affections or intentions. Perhaps only in dressing Kennicott's body for burial did anyone learn of his heart's desire. Once his coat covered the shirt sleeves, no one saw the ribbons. Who dressed Kennicott? Who was a confidant? Who would have kept his secret? Pease, his friend from childhood.

Pease probably knew about the young lady, too, because Kennicott had been entertained many times in her home in San Francisco. She was Olga Klinkofstrom, daughter of the Russian consul. Kennicott was invited to their home often in the four months he stayed in the city. In the Victorian custom, he couldn't have gone to her home alone but neither he nor Pease left any record of what they did in San Francisco. Dall records going with Kennicott to the Klinkofstroms for dinner and entertainment and then only on dates that fall after Rothrock has left town, making it look as though only officers were invited. Dall notes in his diary that Olga is a very pretty girl who plays the piano and sings very nicely, providing everyone with pleasant evenings. He even refers to her as "Bob's friend Olga."[3]

Shortly before the group left San Francisco, a letter Kennicott wrote Baird on July 9, 1865, contained a most unusual post script. He asked what Baird would think of his forming a Russian alliance, alluding to the Russian offer to sell the Yukon Territory, and mentioning that Consul Klinkofstrom has a charming daughter named Olga. Then, in a very boyish way, he admonished Baird, "Don't you tell on me, tho!" [underlined in original] adding, "I don't know and hardly dare suppose she cares a fig for me — but — well Russian alliances are apropos for Americans just now — Anyway I've some pleasant memories to take to the Arctic with me...."[4] If Kennicott was able to talk to her about his feelings, she may have given a noncommittal answer. Thus,

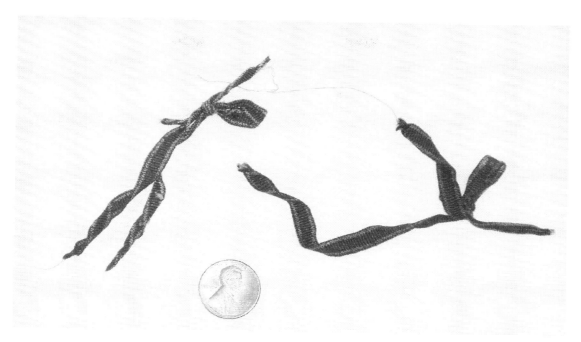

the open lover's knot.

The ribbons from Kennicott's sleeves, enlarged to show open knots.

When Kennicott's body arrived in San Francisco, it's possible that Pease, recognizing the need for a new casket, went to the Klinkofstroms and told of the lover's knots on Kennicott's sleeves. Olga was either shocked to think that a man she was simply nice to cared so much for her, or she was still grieving over the death of the man who was going to come back to her. In either case, the diplomatic family may have been willing to see that such a man, who was also a noted scientist, was sent home in the finest casket available.

It's also possible that Olga saw Robert one last time through the casket's view plate.

Epilogue

What became of the Scientific Corps?

HENRY BANNISTER was hired in 1867 by Baird to unpack and catalog at the Smithsonian the specimens collected in Russian America. Because he had taught himself Russian at St. Michael's, he was asked to translate some articles and documents for the Senate then considering whether to purchase that territory. He also testified before the Senate Committee on Foreign Relations, telling what he could about the land, the animals, and the natives. Returning to Evanston, Illinois, he transferred his scientific interests to medicine, and wrote on mental health and nervous disorders. He died in 1920.

FERDINAND BISCHOFF was hired in 1867 to unpack and catalog the Russian American specimens at the Smithsonian and he testified about his year at Sitka before the Senate Committee on Foreign Relations. At Baird's request, he returned twice to the Arctic areas to collect natural history specimens. Years later, around 1872, he went into the southwestern deserts on a collecting expedition for the Smithsonian and disappeared.

WILLIAM DALL remained in Russian America, collecting specimens and recording data, for a year after it was purchased by the US. In 1868, he returned to Washington and from there conducted various surveys on behalf of the government. Because of his many subsequent northern expeditions, he became known as the Dean of Alaskan Explorations. He died in 1927.

HENRY ELLIOTT spent many years in Alaska living among the natives, applying his drawing skills to depict the daily life of various native tribes. He was one of the first conservationists, protesting the clubbing of seal cubs for their fur on the Pribilof Islands. His lifetime as an environmentalist resulted in his helping to formulate, in 1911, the first international treaty on the conservation of wildlife. He died in 1930.

CHARLES PEASE, JR. returned directly to his family in Cleveland, Ohio, in 1867. His grandfather, Kirtland, wrote Baird that Pease thought the port of Sitka alone would be worth the purchase price for Russian America. Kirtland also wrote members of Congress, reciting the favorable characteristics of his grandson and asking for a position for him in Washington. Pease remained in Cleveland and died in 1875.

GEORGE MAYNARD continued his art studies and later designed and painted scenes on the hallways of the Capitol in Washington, DC. He helped evaluate and supervise the art installed at the 1893 World's Columbian Exposition in Chicago. He died in 1923.

JOSEPH ROTHROCK returned to his home in Pennsylvania in 1866 where he continued to work in the field of botany. He served as Pennsylvania's first commissioner of forestry, becoming known for his emphasis on environmental protection. He died in 1922.

GEORGE ADAMS returned to the Arctic as a fur trader for several years, then became a mining engineer in areas such as Siberia and most of the countries of Europe, Asia, and Africa, particularly the southern Congo. He died in 1938.

What became of the scientific collections?

Spencer Fullerton Baird waited anxiously for the "enormous quantity" of specimens that Bannister reported had been packed and shipped in December 1866 in San Francisco. The twenty-eight boxes finally arrived in late February 1867; both Bannister and Bischoff were hired to unpack and catalog them. The collection, as a group, was acknowledged as "very extensive and valuable" in the Smithsonian Institution's 1867 Annual Report. In the Registrar's files at the Smithsonian's National Museum of Natural History, the specimens for 1866 and 1867 are listed under "Bulkley, Charles S." For 1866, the Registrar's description is "Collections of Russian Telegraph Expedition in various departments of natural history, made by Robert Kennicott, Dr. Fisher, Capt. Sands, Capt. Scammon, W. H. Dall, Henry Bannister and J. T. Rothrock." Dall records that he sent fifteen large boxes in January 1866, "containing 10,000 specimens of all descriptions" collected on the trip to St. Michael's and back.

In 1867, under Bulkley's name, with Kennicott and Dall given in parentheses, the registry lists "28 boxes of collection of the Russian Overland Telegraph Expedition, in all branches of natural history, collected in part by Bischoff, at Sitka." Bannister is credited with "General Collections;" Pease with one item. Bischoff, who collected thirty-one boxes of specimens at Sitka, received no separate listing. Other men — Blake, Cotter, Fletcher, Haining, Huson, Kelsey, Ketchum, Lemon, Scammon, E. E. Smith, Townsend, Whymper — are listed as contributors, primarily of one item each.

The full extent and value of the year spent collecting specimens in the Yukon can be learned by checking the catalogued items in the separate departments of natural history. For example, the mammal collection alone lists forty-two items from men in the Western Union expedition. In addition, ninety-seven birds are attributed to Bischoff. An Arctic hare is attributed to Kennicott, who essentially gave up collecting, as he said he had.

Unfortunately, Kennicott's name as a naturalist and scientist dimmed in his home town because many of the specimens he collected and curated at the Chicago Academy of Sciences were destroyed in a fire at the building on June 7, 1866, a month after Kennicott's death.

Kennicott's Owl

A specimen of this western screech owl was collected by Ferdinand Bischoff in the Sitka area and sent to the Chicago Academy of Sciences where it was studied by Daniel Elliott who recognized it as a new species and named it after Robert Kennicott in 1867. The drawing was done by Henry W. Elliott for William H. Dall's book, *Alaska and Its Resources*.

Acknowledgements

First of all, my thanks to the scientists: Doug Owsley whose invitation to "read papers" caused this information to be collected; Art Aufderheide who answered my naïve questions with good humor; and Grove Director Steve Swanson who was endlessly patient.

With grateful acknowledgement of the generous help from:

All the responsive and resourceful archivists and librarians without whom I'd still be stumbling in the dark. Tracy Robinson, Bill Cox, and especially Ellen Alers eagerly shared the Smithsonian's shelves-full of Kennicott material. Pam Henson, head of Institutional History at the Smithsonian encouraged publication. Patrick Quinn and Janet Olson at Northwestern University answered all requests with impressive speed.

Catherine Hawks, Jeremy Jacobs, Igor Krupnik, Shelly Foote, and Lorie Burgess at SI Natural History. Hal Wallace and Barney Finn at SI American History.

Lorin Ottlinger and Kris Van Voorhis, Grove staff members.

Eleanor Joyner who began decoding Bannister and allowed me to think cracking the code was possible.

Andrew Durney, City Treasurer, and Loni Sipary, historian at Nulato, Alaska.

Jon Austin, Director of the Museum of Funeral Customs, Springfield, Il.

Terry Reimer, Director of Research, National Museum of Civil War Medicine, Winchester, VA.

And the uncounted numbers of people who, just by doing their jobs well, made my search through the past a lot easier and much more fun.

With heartfelt thanks to my friends and accomplices, Johanna Halford-MacLeod and Adrienne Bradford, who kept insisting that I had to turn all this information into something permanent. And to Vicki Simon whose help obtaining images was invaluable.

Above all, my loving thanks to my long-suffering family, for whom Robert Kennicott became a temporary son and brother.

Appendices

Pease's letter to his family

Medical Supplies

Scientific Supplies

Scientific Corps Flag

Letter from Charles Pease to his family as printed in the Chicago Tribune on Saturday, October 27, 1866

Fort St. Michaels. August 19, 1866

My Dear Wife and Parents:

Poor Kennicott is no longer with us. He died suddenly at Nulato, a Russian fort on the Youkon River, the 13th of last May. The facts are these: He had many disappointments and failures since our arrival at St. Michaels, which, though it has been impossible to remedy, had taken a severe hold on him and seemed to have entirely broken him down. He complained much of dizziness and a strange sensation in the head. On the morning of the 13th of May, we had a late breakfast and not seeing Major Kennicott around, concluded he had gone out for a walk as he very often did early in the morning. I sent one of our Indians to look for him. Lebarge, one of our party, and I took a walk down the river bank and had not gone over two hundred yards from the fort when I saw Kennicott lying on his back; I ran up to him and saw in an instant that he was dead. I sent Lebarge back for assistance which immediately came and conveyed the body to the fort. An open compass was lying by his side. It is supposed he was taking bearings, and after learning over and making marks on the sand, raised up and then fell over dead. I cannot describe the feelings of our party. There were six of us at Nulato at the time of Major Kennicott's death, waiting for the ice in the river to break up so that we could start in boats for Fort Youkon, a distance of six hundred miles.

Mr. Ketchum, the oldest one of the party, takes command. He appointed me second in command, and desired me to do with the remains of Major Kennicott as I thought proper. I employed a Russian to make a coffin, which was rendered perfectly tight with spruce pitch procured from the Indians. We placed the remains in the coffin and kept it open for three days, when we took our last look, and then deposited it in a vault, as I decided to take the remains to St. Michaels, a distance of five hundred miles by river, and eighty miles from the mouth of the river by sea. In the winter we cross over the mountains with our dogs and sleds; by that route it is only two hundred and fifty miles, but it was then too late for the latter route, as the mountain streams were fast breaking up, so I decided to start down the river as soon as the ice broke up. We had two Esquimaux boats made of seal skins, that we had intended to have gone to Fort Youkon in. I took the largest one, which is thirty-three feet long and six feet wide, and rigged with a large sail. On the 23rd of May the ice broke up; on the morning of the 25th we loaded the boat with things necessary for the trip, and then placed the Major's remains on board. We bade good-bye to Messrs. Ketchum and Lebarge who started the next day for Fort Youkon. Accompanying me were Messrs. Smith, Adams, and Dyer. For a crew I had three Indians. After sailing down the river a few miles from Nulato we overtook the ice and drift wood and found a very rapid current and it seemed every moment as though the boat would swamp, but we managed to land on an island and while there had a heavy thunder shower. About 8 p.m. we started again and ran about twenty miles when we camped for the night. Next day we made about fifty miles, passed an Indian village called Khottog, stopped there a few minutes and bought some fish of the Indians. At night camped on an island; 27th, travelled about thirteen miles, came to an Indian village containing about one hundred Indians. Engaged one to go with Dyer, who left us there and went across to Unalakleat, where the other party had been stopping. 28th, left at one a.m., had fair wind all day, stopped once, then continued until twelve at night. The current was very rapid, with large quantities of drift wood, but little ice. We made about seventy-seven miles. 29th, left camp early in the morning – passed an Indian village. They fired guns for us to stop, but were a ------- from shore and kept on our course. Shortly after, we met about fifty Esquimaux with their boats going up the river on a trading expedition. We stopped a short time and had a talk with them. I had seen many of them in the winter at Unalakleat. I informed them of Major Kennicott's death, which affected them very much, as he had been a great favorite with them all.

June 6th, started with fair wind and tide, stood out to sea about six miles to clear some long points, sailed forty miles and at evening put into a small river and took tea, started out again and at four in the morning entered the channel leading direct to Fort St. Michaels. Early in the morning of the 15th, we were within sight of the fort but the channel was very shallow and rocky and we were obliged to proceed very slow. When near the fort we fired a gun which brought all the party to the beach to meet us. Dyer went to Unalakleat and informed the party that we were on the way down with the remains of Major Kennicott, and they came here. In the afternoon we had a funeral service, and deposited the remains in a vault where they will remain until the arrival of the ship, when I hope they will be sent home. I shall do all in my power to have them forwarded.

Note: No diary or report from Pease has been located. The dates and information in this letter correlate closely with the information in Adams's diary. Pease's third sentence, beginning with "The facts are these" is taken almost directly from Adams's diary. Most likely, this letter is not a third account of the river trip, complementing Smith's and Adams's, but a retelling of Adams.

List of Medical Supplies furnished Lieut. Wm. H. Dall

For use of party to which he is appointed Acting Medical Officer (Flag Ship "Nightingale" Off Redoubt St. Michael, September 27, 1866)

1# ground mustard
1# Epsom salts
2# flax seed
1# simple cerate [waxy substance to coat the skin]
1/2# blistering ointment
1/4# mercurial ointment
1 botl wine pepsine [digestive]
1 botl cherry pectoral [coughs,colds]
unreadable (perhaps 1/2 ? Sensen Leaves)
unreadable (perhaps ½ ? Bicarb Soda)
6 oz Peruvian bark [yields quinine and other alkaloids]
6 oz finch catechu [astringent substances from East Indian acacia trees]
4 oz citrate magnesiu [antacid and laxative]
2 oz pulv rhubarb [combined cathartic and astringent]
1 oz pulv kusso [flowers of Ethiopian tree used for expelling tapeworms]
4 oz Barbour's mixture [digestive]
4 oz laudanum [narcotic]
4 oz extract ginger
4 oz spirits camphor [for pain and itching]
4 oz castor oil
4 oz opodeldoc [liniments containing soap, camphor, alcohol, etc]
2 oz elixir vitriol [aromatic sulfuric acid; scurvey treatment]
1 oz spirits lavender [relieves flatulence]
1 oz arnica [a wound dressing]
1 oz peppermint
1 oz Fryars Balsam [aromatic, soothing ointment]
½ oz kreosote [preservative, antiseptic]
½ oz oil cloves [toothache]
1/8 oz morphia sulph.
1 oz pulv. Kino [like catechu]
1 oz pulv. Alum [astringent and styptic] unreadable
1 oz sugar lead [lead acetate; digestive complaints]
½ oz powdered nitre [potassium nitrate; fuming inhalant]
½ oz monsills salts
1 oz nitrate silver [gonorrhea]
2 oz gum Arabic [constipation]
200 pills cal & jalap 5 gr
200 pills doveri 3 gr. [Dover's powder containing ipecac and opium used as an anodyne, diaphoretic, and antispasmodic]
100 pills opii 1 gr
100 pills quinine 1 gr
100 pills purgative
10 powder Ipecac 15 gr [emetic]
10 pills Cal & jalep 10 gr

SIA, RU 7073, Wm. H. Dall Papers, Box 18, Folder 6

Medicines on hand at Fort St. Michael's, 1865

cathartic pills - 10
emetic powders
dover powders
C & O pills
quinine - 10
R. R. R. -10 - 10 -
Ginger Ess. -10 - 10 -
kreosote - 10-
glycerine Liniments 10 salts 10
sticking plasters & Russia salve -10-
paragoric -10-
camphor -10 - 10
Brandy or Whisky, a moderate
   amount for medical purposes.

Northwestern University Archives, Robert Kennicott-Henry M. Bannister Papers, Series 11/2/2; Box 1, Folder 6, Bannister Journal

List of Stores
Received by Robert Kennicott

For Youkon Expedition from H. M. Bannister Ass't StoreKeeper in charge of Scientific Stores at St. Michael's R.A. on the 22nd day of September 1865.

 6 nests pill boxes
 400 fish bags
 1 lot drawing paper
 1 lot Indian vocabularies
 3 large pocket knives
 2 scissors
 3 pair forceps
 3 pamphlets directions
 4 geological hammers
 5 lbs shot (Stipanoff)
 4 botanical straps
 2 dozen common buckles
 1 dozen patent buckles
 4 drawing boards
 1 soldering iron
 1 lb solder
 1 rubber gas bag
 9 blow pipes
 16 egg drills
 20 lbs arsenic
 50 lbs (10 cans) saltpeter & alum
 5 empty cans
 2 alcohol chests
 2 copper tanks
 2 gals alcohol
 1 pkg tissue paper
 12 geological chisels
 1 lot wrapping paper

Northwestern University Archives, Robert Kennicott-Henry M. Bannister Papers, Series 11/2/2; Box 1, Folder 6, Bannister Journal

Scientific supplies furnished each vessel

 (*Palmetto, Clara Bell, Onward, Golden Gate, Rutgers*)
 6 quires botanical paper
 2 lbs arsenic in cans
 1 notebook, 100 labels
 16 pill boxes
 25 fish bags
 Six bottles asst sizes corked & filled with alcohol pure

SIA, RU 7073, Wm. H. Dall Papers, Box 2, Scrapbook

The Scientific Corps Flag

Before the Yukon-bound Scientific Corps left San Francisco in June 1865, Dall showed Kennicott his design for shoulder straps and a cap medallion that he would wear as Scientific Director of Natural History. Dall's area of scientific expertise was shells and marine life so he chose scallop shells for his shoulders and a gold bug for his cap. The next month, as they all were in route to St. Michaels, he decided: "must get up a scientific flag for my boat." It's not clear what boat he meant since he knew he wouldn't be staying in the Yukon.

By July 31, aboard the *Golden Gate*, he had "designed a flag for the Scientific Corps" which he described as "a blue cross and narrow border on a white field with a white Pecten (scallop shell) in the center. It will be quite neat. Painted the Scallop for the flag." Bannister, Bischoff and Pease were also on the *Gate* and may have seen the flag as Dall worked on it or when he finished painting and sewing it on August 4. At that time, Kennicott was aboard the *Wright* and could not have been asked for his approval when the flag was being made. It is not clear whether Kennicott ever saw Dall's flag.

Dall created his flag shortly before Bischoff was left in Sitka to recover from his blistered hands and long after Rothrock, Maynard, and Elliott left San Francisco to go through British Columbia. None of them could have used the flag. Dall may have left the flag at St. Michael's but, though Adams mentions flying the US flag at the bow of his boat as he started up the Yukon, he does not mention a flying a Scientific Corps flag. Nor do the other men based with Kennicott — Smith, Bannister, Pease — mention such a flag.

Based on drawings in his diary, Dall flew his flag at Unalacleet and at Nulato when he took over after Kennicott's death. Since Dall was now Director of the Scientific Corps, technically his creation can be designated as the flag of the Scientific Corps. But it is doubtful whether any of the other members of the Scientific Corps of the Western Union Telegraph Expedition used it.

Notes

Abbreviation used throughout for Smithsonian Institution Archives, Record Unit: SIA, RU

Autopsy

[1] W. H. Deppermann, "Two Cents an Acre," *The North American Review*, Vol. 245, No. 1 (Spring, 1938): 126-133

[2] George Adams, *Life on the Yukon, 1865-1867*, (Kingston, Ontario: Limestone Press, 1982). 91

[3] SIA, RU 7002, Spencer Fullerton Baird Papers, 1833-1889, Box 33, folder 28

Grove Archives

[1] *Transactions of the Chicago Academy of Sciences*, Vol. I, Pt. II, (Chicago: The Academy, 1869). 133

Notes 2 - 6: The Grove Archives, Glenview Park District, Glenview, Il., Kennicott Family Letters

Chicago 1864

[1] SIA, RU 7002 Spencer Fullerton Baird Papers, 1833-1889, Box 27, folder 5

[2] W. H. Dall, *Spencer Fullerton Baird: A Biography*, (Philadelphia: J.B. Lippincott Company, 1915). 369

[3] SIA, RU 7002, Spencer Fullerton Baird Papers, 1833-1889, Box 27, folder 7

[4] SIA, RU 7213, Western Union Telegraph Expedition Collection, 1865-1867, Box 1, Bulkley folder

[5] SIA, RU 7002, Spencer Fullerton Baird Papers, 1833-1889, Box 27, folder 7

[6] SIA, RU 7002, Spencer Fullerton Baird Papers, 1833-1889, Box 27, folder 8

[7] SIA, RU 7073, Wm. H. Dall Papers, Box 20, diaries

[8] SIA, RU 7213, Western Union Telegraph Expedition Collection, 1865-1867, Box 1, Kennicott folder

[9] SIA, RU 7002, Spencer Fullerton Baird Papers, 1833-1889, Box 27, folder 8

[10] *www.150si.edu/chap3/three/htm* [Smithsonian Institution]

[11] *Transactions of the Chicago Academy of Sciences*, Vol. I, Pt. II, (Chicago: The Academy, 1869). 140

Spring 1865

[1] Northwestern University Archives, Robert Kennicott-Henry M. Bannister Papers, Series 11/2/2, Box 2

Notes 2, 3, 4: SIA, RU 7073, Wm. H. Dall Papers, Box 20, diaries

[5] SIA, RU 7002, Spencer Fullerton Baird Papers, 1833-1889, Box 27, folder 7

[6] SIA, RU 7213, Western Union Telegraph Expedition Collection, 1865-1867, Box 1, Bulkley folder

[7] SIA, RU 7213, Western Union Telegraph Expedition Collection, 1865-1867, Box 1, Clippings folder

[8] Northwestern University Archives, Robert Kennicott-Henry M. Bannister Papers, Series 11/2/2, Box 2

[9] SIA, RU 7001, Joseph Henry Collection, Division 4, Box 4, folder 1

[10] SIA, RU 7073, Wm. H. Dall Papers, Box 20, diaries

[11] SIA, RU 7073, Wm. H. Dall Papers, Box 20, diaries

[12] James Alton James, *The First Scientific Exploration of Russian America and the Purchase of Alaska*, (Evanston, Il.: Northwestern University, 1942). 140

[13] SIA, RU 7213, Western Union Telegraph Expedition Collection, 1865-1867, Box 1, Kennicott folder

[14] The Conservation Fund, *Ecological and Cultural Significance of the MacArthur Foundation's Property at The Grove*, (Glenview, Il.: The Grove, 1995). 46

[15] SIA, RU 7213, Western Union Telegraph Expedition Collection, 1865-1867, Box 1, Kennicott folder

[16] SIA, RU 7073, Wm. H. Dall Papers, Box 20, diaries

[17] SIA, RU 7073, Wm. H. Dall Papers, Box 20, diaries

[18] SIA, RU 7073, Wm. H. Dall Papers, Box 2, Dall folder

[19] James Alton James, *The First Scientific Exploration of Russian America and the Purchase of Alaska*, (Evanston, Il.: Northwestern University, 1942). 143

Strychnine

[1] *http://www.homeopathy-canada.com*, The Toronto School of Homeopathic Medicine

[2] *http://www.minutus.org*, American Medical College of Homeopathy, *Hahnemann's Materia Medica Pura*

[3] *http://www.minutus.org*, American Medical College of Homeopathy, *Hahnemann's Materia Medica Pura*

[4] The Grove Archives, Glenview Park District, Glenview, Il., Kennicott Family Letters

[5] *Transactions of the Chicago Academy of Sciences*, Vol. I, Pt. II, (Chicago: The Academy, 1869). 175

[6] SIA, RU 7002, Spencer Fullerton Baird Papers, 1833-1889, Box 26, Kennicott folder

http://www.henriettasherbal.com provided digital versions of:

[7] Samuel O. L. Potter, *Handbook of Materia Medica,Pharmacy, and Therapeutics*, (Philadelphia: P. Blakiston, Scon & Co., 1890)

[8] Harvey Wickes Felter, John Uri Lloyd, *King's American Dispensatory*, third revision, eighteenth edition, 1898

[9] Samuel L. Potter, *A Compendium of Materia Medica*, 1902

[10] *http://www.inchem.org*, International Programme on Chemical Safety, Canada

San Francisco, Spring 1865

[1] The Progress of the Electric Telegraph, *Atlantic Monthly*, Vol. 16, No. 97, November 1865

[2] The Overland European Telegraph, *New York Times*, February 15, 1865 from the *Alta Californian*, January 22, 1865

[3] The Overland Telegraph, *New York Times*, October 29, 1866

[4] SIA, RU 7213, Western Union Telegraph Expedition Collection, 1865-1867, Box 1, Clippings folder

[5] The Russo-American Telegraph, *New York Times*, August 13, 1865 from *San Francisco Bulletin*, July 11, 1865

[6] SIA, RU 7002, Spencer Fullerton Baird Papers, 1833-1889, Box 27, folder 7

[7] SIA, RU 7213, Western Union Telegraph Expedition Collection, 1865-1867, Box 1, Kennicott folder

[8] SIA, RU 7213, Western Union Telegraph Expedition Collection, 1865-1867, Box 1, Kennicott folder

[9] *http://www.telegraphtrail.org/history*, ©2002 Dwight Dodge, Letter from Ralph Pope to *Berkshire Courier*, Great Barrington, MA

[10] SIA, RU 7213, Western Union Telegraph Expedition Collection, 1865-1867, Box 1, Kennicott folder

[11] SIA, RU 7213, Western Union Telegraph Expedition Collection, 1865-1867, Box 1, Kennicott folder

[12] SIA, RU 7073, Wm. H. Dall Papers, Box 20, diaries

[13] SIA, RU 7213, Western Union Telegraph Expedition Collection, 1865-1867, Box 1, Dall folder

[14] SIA, RU 7213, Western Union Telegraph Expedition Collection, 1865-1867, Box 1, Kennicott folder

Notes 15, 16, 17: SIA, RU 7073, Wm. H. Dall Papers, Box 20, diaries

Notes 18 - 21: SIA, RU 7213, Western Union Telegraph Expedition Collection, 1865-1867, Box 1, Kennicott folder

[22] SIA, RU 7073, Wm. H. Dall Papers, Box 20, diaries

[23] SIA, RU 7073, Wm. H. Dall Papers, Box 1, folder 11

[24] *Transactions of the Chicago Academy of Sciences*, Vol. I, Pt. II, (Chicago: The Academy, 1869). 219

[25] SIA, RU 7002, Spencer Fullerton Baird Papers, 1833-1889, Box 27, folder 8

[26] SIA, RU 7213, Western Union Telegraph Expedition Collection, 1865-1867, Box 1, Kennicott folder

[27] SIA, RU 7213, Western Union Telegraph Expedition Collection, 1865-1867, Box 1, Kennicott folder

Pulseless Faint

[1] SIA, RU 7213, Western Union Telegraph Expedition Collection, 1865-1867, Box 1, Dall folder

San Francisco, Summer 1865

Notes 1, 2, 3: SIA, RU 7213, Western Union Telegraph Expedition Collection, 1865-1867, Box 1, Kennicott folder

[4] The National Fast, The Calamity and the Blessing, *New York Times*, June 1, 1865

[5] SIA, RU 7213, Western Union Telegraph Expedition Collection, 1865-1867, Box 1, Kennicott folder

[6] SIA, RU 7073, Wm. H. Dall Papers, Box 20, diaries

[7] SIA, RU 7073, Wm. H. Dall Papers, Box 18

[8] George Adams, *Life on the Yukon, 1865-1867*, (Kingston, Ontario: Limestone Press, 1982). 15

[9] SIA, RU 7213, Western Union Telegraph Expedition Collection, 1865-1867, Box 1, Dall folder

[10] SIA, RU 7073, Wm. H. Dall Papers, Box 20, diaries

[11] SIA, RU 7073, Wm. H. Dall Papers, Box 2

[12] Wm. H. Dall, *Spencer Fullerton Baird: A Biography*, (Philadelphia: J.B. Lippincott Company, 1915). 232

Notes 13, 14, 15: SIA, RU 7073, Wm. H. Dall Papers, Box 20, diaries

[16] Smithsonian Institution Archives Center, National Museum of American History, Western Union Telegraph Company, series 2, Subsidiaries 1844-1985, Collection 205, Box 119A

[17] SIA, RU 7213, Western Union Telegraph Expedition Collection, 1865-1867, Box 1, Bulkley folder

Transactions

[1] *Transactions of the Chicago Academy of Sciences*, Vol. I, Pt. II, (Chicago: The Academy, 1869). 216

[2] SIA, RU 7073, Wm. H. Dall Papers, Box 1, folder 10

To the Yukon, Summer 1865

[1] SIA, RU 7073, Wm. H. Dall Papers, Box 20, diaries

Notes 2 - 6: SIA, RU 7213, Western Union Telegraph Expedition Collection, 1865-1867, Box 1, Kennicott folder

Notes 7, 8, 9: SIA, RU 7073, Wm. H. Dall Papers, Box 20, diaries

[10] SIA, RU 7073, Wm. H. Dall Papers, Box 12, folder 33

[11] The Pirate Shenandoah, *New York Times*, August 27, 1865

[12] SIA, RU 7213, Western Union Telegraph Expedition Collection, 1865-1867, Box 1, Kennicott folder

[13] SIA, RU 7002, Spencer Fullerton Baird Papers, 1833-1889, Box 27, folder 8

[14] The Grove Archives, Glenview Park District, Glenview, Il., Kennicott Family Letters

[15] SIA, RU 7073 William H. Dall Papers, Box 1, folder 11

[16] SIA, RU 7213, Western Union Telegraph Expedition Collection, 1865-1867, Box 1, Dall folder

[17] *Transactions of the Chicago Academy of Sciences*, Vol. I, Pt. II, (Chicago: The Academy, 1869). 186

[18] SIA, RU 7073, William H. Dall Papers, Box 1

[19] University of Washington Manuscript Special Collection & University Archives Division, Western Union Telegraph Co. Diaries, Charles S. Hubble Collection, Frederick M. Smith Diary, unpaginated

[20] SIA, RU 7073, Wm. H. Dall Papers, Box 20, diaries

[21] University of Washington Manuscript Special Collection & University Archives Division, Western Union Telegraph Co. Diaries, Charles S. Hubble Collection, Frederick M. Smith Diary, unpaginated

[22] James Alton James, *The First Scientific Exploration of Russian America and the Purchase of Alaska*, (Evanston, Il.: Northwestern University, 1942). 175

St. Michaels, Fall 1865

[1] SIA, RU 7213, Western Union Telegraph Expedition Collection, 1865-1867, Box 1, Kennicott folder

[2] SIA, RU 7073, Wm. H. Dall Papers, Box 20, diaries

[3] SIA, RU 7213, Western Union Telegraph Expedition Collection, 1865-1867, Box 1, Bannister folder

[4] *Transactions of the Chicago Academy of Sciences*, Vol. I, Pt. II, (Chicago: The Academy, 1869). 220

[5] *Transactions of the Chicago Academy of Sciences*, Vol. I, Pt. II, (Chicago: The Academy, 1869). 220

[6] University of Washington Manuscript Special Collection & University Archives Division, Western Union Telegraph Co. Diaries, Charles S. Hubble Collection, Frederick M. Smith Diary, unpaginated

[7] SIA, RU 7213, Western Union Telegraph Expedition Collection, 1865-1867, Box 1, Bannister folder

[8] SIA, RU 7213, Western Union Telegraph Expedition Collection, 1865-1867, Box 1, Kennicott folder

[9] SIA, RU 7213, Western Union Telegraph Expedition Collection, 1865-1867, Box 1, folder 1

[10] *http://www.buchholdt.com/St.Michael/antonson.html*, Joan M. Antonson, *St. Michael: Alaska's Western Crossroads*

[11] James Alton James, *The First Scientific Exploration of Russian America and the Purchase of Alaska*, (Evanston, Il.: Northwestern University, 1942). 268

[12] SIA, RU 7073, Wm. H. Dall Papers, Box 20, diaries

Unalacleet and Nulato, Winter 1865-66

[1] James Alton James, *The First Scientific Exploration of Russian America and the Purchase of Alaska*, (Evanston, Il.: Northwestern University, 1942). 268

[2] Frederick Whymper, *Travel and Adventure in the Territory of Alaska*, (London: J. Murray, 1868). 135

[3] James Alton James, *The First Scientific Exploration of Russian America and the Purchase of Alaska*, (Evanston, Il.: Northwestern University, 1942). 268

[4] SIA, RU 7213, Western Union Telegraph Expedition Collection, 1865-1867, Box 1, Kennicott folder

[5] The Western Union diarists reflect the social structure of their time by not identifying most of the natives and Russians on whose invaluable help they constantly relied. From various diary entries, it seems the Western Union men always traveled with several natives to guide them, prepare their camp, and cook their food.

[6] George Adams, *Life on the Yukon, 1865-1867*, (Kingston, Ontario: Limestone Press, 1982). 129

[7] George Adams, *Life on the Yukon, 1865-1867*, (Kingston, Ontario: Limestone Press, 1982). 129

[8] SIA, RU 7073, Wm. H. Dall Papers, Box 2, scrapbook

[9] James Alton James, *The First Scientific Exploration of Russian America and the Purchase of Alaska*, (Evanston, Il.: Northwestern University, 1942). 267

[10] James Alton James, *The First Scientific Exploration of Russian America and the Purchase of Alaska*, (Evanston, Il.: Northwestern University, 1942). 269

[11] George Adams, *Life on the Yukon, 1865-1867*, (Kingston, Ontario: Limestone Press, 1982). 142

[12] SIA, RU 7213, Western Union Telegraph Expedition Collection, 1865-1867, Box 1, Ennis folder

[13] George Adams, *Life on the Yukon, 1865-1867*, (Kingston, Ontario: Limestone Press, 1982). 146

Nulato, Winter 1866

[1] SIA, RU 7073, Wm. H. Dall Papers, Box 18, folder 12

[2] George Adams, *Life on the Yukon, 1865-1867*, (Kingston, Ontario: Limestone Press, 1982). 135

[3] SIA, RU 7073, Wm. H. Dall Papers, Box 18, folder 12

[4] SIA, RU 7073, Wm. H. Dall Papers, Box 18, folder 12

[5] SIA, RU 7073, Wm. H. Dall Papers, Box 20, folder 1

[6] SIA, RU 7073, Wm. H. Dall Papers, Box 18, folder 12

[7] George Adams, *Life on the Yukon, 1865-1867*, (Kingston, Ontario: Limestone Press, 1982). 151

[8] SIA, RU 7073, Wm. H. Dall Papers, Box 18, folder 11

Notes 9 - 14: SIA, RU 7073, Wm. H. Dall Papers, Box 18, folder 12

[15] SIA, RU 7073, Wm. H. Dall Papers, Box 2

[16] SIA, RU 7073, Wm. H. Dall Papers, Box 18, folder 12

[17] SIA, RU 7073, Wm. H. Dall Papers, Box 18, folder 12

[18] SIA, RU 7073, Wm. H. Dall Papers, Box 18, folder 14

[19] George Adams, *Life on the Yukon, 1865-1867*, (Kingston, Ontario: Limestone Press, 1982). 160

[20] SIA, RU 7002, Spencer Fullerton Baird Papers, Box 18, folder 21

[21] University of Washington Manuscript Special Collection & University Archives Division, Western Union Telegraph Co. Diaries, Charles S. Hubble Collection, Frederick M. Smith Diary, unpaginated

Russian Rescue

[1] University of Washington Manuscript Special Collection & University Archives Division, Western Union Telegraph Co. Diaries, Charles S. Hubble Collection, Frederick M. Smith Diary, unpaginated

[2] *Transactions of the Chicago Academy of Sciences*, Vol. I, Pt. II, (Chicago: The Academy, 1869). 222

Lead and Arsenic

[1] Arthur C. Aufderheide, M. D. and Larry Cartmell, M. D., *Report on the Autopsy and Laboratory Studies on Robert Kennicott*, May 2001

Nulato, May 1866

[1] These statements are reported by Dall in *Transactions*; the letters themselves are not available. Adams confirms that various papers were found among Kennicott's things.

[2] George Adams, *Life on the Yukon, 1865-1867*, (Kingston, Ontario: Limestone Press, 1982). 160

[3] In 1867 Dall wrote Baird an account of finding Kennicott's body that matches the

account of Adams. Dall's account in *Transactions* presents a different version.

4 University of Washington Manuscript Special Collection & University Archives Division, Western Union Telegraph Co. Diaries, Charles S. Hubble Collection, Frederick M. Smith Diary, unpaginated

5 University of Washington Manuscript Special Collection & University Archives Division, Western Union Telegraph Co. Diaries, Charles S. Hubble Collection, Frederick M. Smith Diary, unpaginated

6 Pease's grandfather, Jared Kirtland, confused Kennicott's two burial places when he wrote to the *New York Times* saying that Lt. Bernard's "...remains are now preserved by the Russians in a vault excavated in frozen earth at St. Michael's. In this vault Kennicott's remains were deposited till late in September." [*NYT*, May 21, 1867] Kirtland may have wanted to associate Kennicott with the Franklin Expedition, and Kennicott's remains were in the St. Michael's vault, but Bernard's were in the Nulato permafrost where Kennicott was initially buried.

7 University of Washington Manuscript Special Collection & University Archives Division, Western Union Telegraph Co. Diaries, Charles S. Hubble Collection, Frederick M. Smith Diary, unpaginated

8 *www.telegraphtrail.org*, ©2002, Dwight Dodge, Letter from J. T. Rothrock to Provincial Librarian and Archivist, Victoria, BC, January 11, 1913

9 SIA, RU 7073, Wm. H. Dall Papers, Box 4

10 SIA, RU 7073, Wm. H. Dall Papers, Box 18

11 SIA, RU 7213, Western Union Telegraph Expedition Collection, 1865-1867, Box 1, Dall folder

Newsworthy Death

1 SIA, RU 7213, Western Union Telegraph Expedition Collection, 1865-1867, Box 1, Clippings folder

2 SIA, RU 52, Spencer Fullerton Baird Correspondence, Box 25, Vol. 33, p. 493

3 SIA, RU 7213, Western Union Telegraph Expedition Collection, 1865-1867, Box 1, Clippings folder

4 SIA, RU 52, Spencer Fullerton Baird Correspondence, Box 25, Vol. 33, p. 495

5 SIA, RU 7213, Western Union Telegraph Expedition Collection, 1865-1867, Box 1, Clippings folder

Fall-Winter, 1866-67

1 James Alton James, *The First Scientific Exploration of Russian America and the Purchase of Alaska*, (Evanston, Il.: Northwestern University, 1942). 236

2 James Alton James, *The First Scientific Exploration of Russian America and the Purchase of Alaska*, (Evanston, Il.: Northwestern University, 1942). 238

3 SIA, RU 7073, Wm. H. Dall Papers, Box 2, folder 2

4 SIA, RU 7073, Wm. H. Dall Papers, Box 2, folder 1

5 SIA, RU 7213, Western Union Telegraph Expedition Collection, 1865-1867, Box 1, Dall folder

6 SIA, RU 7213, Western Union Telegraph Expedition Collection, 1865-1867, Box 2, Bannister folder

7 SIA, RU 7213, Western Union Telegraph Expedition Collection, 1865-1867, Box 1, Clippings folder

8 SIA, RU 53, Spencer Fullerton Baird Correspondence, Vol. 36, p. 205

9 SIA, RU 7213, Western Union Telegraph Expedition Collection, 1865-1867, Box 1, Clippings folder

10 SIA, RU 7213, Western Union Telegraph Expedition Collection, 1865-1867, Box 1, Clippings folder

11 SIA, RU 7002, Spencer Fullerton Baird Papers, 1833-1889, Box 33, folder 28

12 SIA, RU 7213, Western Union Telegraph Expedition Collection, 1865-1867, Box 1, Clippings folder

13 James Alton James, *The First Scientific Exploration of Russian America and the Pur-*

chase of Alaska, (Evanston, Il.: Northwestern University, 1942). 258

[14] Russian American Telegraph Company, New York Times, December 10, 1866

[15] James Alton James, The First Scientific Exploration of Russian America and the Purchase of Alaska, (Evanston, Il.: Northwestern University, 1942). 260

[16] Daily Evening Bulletin, (San Francisco, CA.), December 22, 1866

[17] SIA, RU 7213, Western Union Telegraph Expedition Collection, 1865-1867, Box 1, Clippings folder

[18] James Alton James, The First Scientific Exploration of Russian America and the Purchase of Alaska, (Evanston, Il.: Northwestern University, 1942). 263

[19] SIA, RU 7002, Spencer Fullerton Baird Papers, 1833-1889, Box 33, folder 28

[20] SIA, RU 7002, Spencer Fullerton Baird Papers, 1833-1889, Box 33, folder 28

[21] The Daily Cleveland Herald, (Cleveland, OH.), January 26, 1867

[22] SIA, RU 7002, Spencer Fullerton Baird Papers, 1833-1889, Box 33, folder 28

[23] The Conservation Fund, Ecological and Cultural Significance of the MacArthur Foundation's Property at The Grove, (Glenview, Il.: The Grove, 1995). 7

[24] SIA, RU 7073, Wm. H. Dall Papers, Box 16

[25] Annual Report of the Board of Regents of the Smithsonian Institution, (Washington, D.C.: Government Printing Office, 1867)

[26] Daily Evening Bulletin, (San Francisco, CA.), January 18, 1867

[27] Daily Inter Ocean, (Chicago, IL), November 22, 1891

[28] Morgan B. Sherwood, Exploration of Alaska, 1865-1900, (New Haven, Conn.: Yale University Press, 1965).

Mercury

[1] http://www.eurekalert.org, "Lincoln's little blue pills," University of Chicago Medical Center, July 17, 2001

[2] Hillary Mayell, "Did Mercury in "Little Blue Pills" Make Abraham Lincoln Erratic?" National Geographic News, July 17, 2001

[3] "Blue No More," Pictures of Health, Fall 2001, Academic Health Center, University of Minnesota, Minneapolis

Kennicott's Death

[1] SIA, RU 7073, Wm. H. Dall Papers, Box 2, folder 1

[2] SIA, RU 7073, Wm. H. Dall Papers, Box 2, folder 2

[3] SIA, RU 7073, Wm. H. Dall Papers, Box 12, folder 1

[4] "Century Old Death Records," New York Times, May 18, 2004, Science section

[5] SIA, RU 33, Spencer Fullerton Baird Correspondence, Vol.78, p. 205

[6] Daily Evening Bulletin, (San Francisco, CA), December 22, 1866

[7] James Alton James, The First Scientific Exploration of Russian America and the Purchase of Alaska, (Evanston, Il.: Northwestern University, 1942). 270

[8] SIA, RU 7213, Western Union Telegraph Expedition Collection, 1865-1867, Box 1, Fisher folder

[9] SIA, RU 7073, Wm. H. Dall Papers, Box 20

[10] SIA, RU 7002, Spencer Fullerton Baird Papers, 1833-1889, Box 27

[11] George Adams, Life on the Yukon, 1865-1867, (Kingston, Ontario: Limestone Press, 1982). 91

[12] Ted C. Hinkley, The Americanization of Alaska, 1867-1897, (Palo Alto, Ca.: Pacific Books, 1972). 192

[13] John B. Dwyer, To Wire the World: Perry M. Collins and the North Pacific Telegraph Expedition, (Westport, Ct.: Praeger, 2000). 105

[14] Arthur C. Aufderheide, M. D. and Larry Cartmell, M. D., *Report on the Autopsy and Laboratory Studies on Robert Kennicott,* May 2001

Kennicott's Preservation

[1] Charles McCurdy, *Embalming and Embalming Fluids* (Wooster, Ohio: Herald Printing Co., 1896).

[2] Paul Fledzic, Personal communication

Decoding Bannister

[1] SIA, RU 7073, Wm. H. Dall Papers, Box 2, folder 1

[2] James Alton James, *The First Scientific Exploration of Russian America and the Purchase of Alaska,* (Evanston, Il.: Northwestern University, 1942). 152

[3] James Alton James, *The First Scientific Exploration of Russian America and the Purchase of Alaska,* (Evanston, Il.: Northwestern University, 1942). 199

Kennicott's Strychnine

[1] Smithsonian Institution Archives Center, National Museum of American History, Western Union Telegraph Company, series 2, Subsidiaries 1844-1985, Collection 205, Box 31

Notes 2-4: SIA, RU 7213, Western Union Telegraph Expedition Collection, 1865-1867, Box 1, Dall folder

Kennicott's Casket

[1] Shelly Foote, Smithsonian Institution, retired, personal communication

[2] Clifford W. Ashley, *The Ashley Book of Knots,* (New York; Doubleday, 1993)

[3] SIA, RU 7213, Western Union Telegraph Expedition Collection, 1865-1867, Box 1, Dall folder

[4] SIA, RU 7213, Western Union Telegraph Expedition Collection, 1865-1867, Box 1, Kennicott folder

Image Credits

Scientist William Healey Dall and artist Frederick Whymper retraced Kennicott's route in 1867 and sketched scenes on their way. Whymper's drawings appear in his book, *Travel and Adventure in the Territory of Alaska*. Dall's diary sketches were more fully drawn by Henry W. Elliott, a fellow WU explorer and Smithsonian scientist, for Dall's book, *Alaska and its Resources*.

P. 8: Kennicott home at The Grove, c. 1996. Photo by Steve Swanson. ©The Grove (Courtesy of The Grove Archives, Glenview Park District, Glenview, Il.)

P. 9 - 12: Photographs taken at the 2001 autopsy of Robert Kennicott. Smithsonian Institution, Chip Clark photographer. (Courtesy of Douglas Owsley, Curator, Anthropology Department, National Museum of Natural History, Smithsonian Institution.)

P. 15: Young Kennicott, c. 1850. (Courtesy of the Smithsonian Institution Archives, RU 95, Photograph Collection, Box 14, folder 39; Neg. # 79-14801)

P. 17: Kennicott home at The Grove, c. 1860. (Courtesy of The Grove Archives, Glenview Park District, Glenview, Il.)

P. 20: Collins Overland Letterhead. (Courtesy of the Smithsonian Institution Archives, RU 7073, Box 18, folder 5; #2005-14096)

P. 22: Telegraph key. (Henry Alexander White, *Beginner's History of the US* (New York: American Book Company, 1906)301. Copyright: 2009, Florida Center for Instructional Technology.)

P. 23: Morse Code. www.artofmanliness.com, 2010

P. 24: Spencer F. Baird, c. 1860. (Courtesy of the Smithsonian Institution Archives, RU 95, Photograph Collection, Box 2, folder 6; Neg. #2004-18872)

P. 26: Robert Kennicott, c. 1860. (Courtesy of The Grove Archives, Glenview Park District, Glenview, Il.)

P. 31: Henry M. Bannister. (Courtesy of the Smithsonian Institution Archives, RU 95, Photograph Collection, Box 3, Folder 9; Neg. # 2004-18873)

P. 31: William H. Dall. (Courtesy of The Grove Archives, Glenview Park District, Glenview, Il.)

P. 32: Charles Pease, Jr. (Courtesy of The Grove Archives, Glenview Park District, Glenview, Il.)

P. 32: George W. Maynard. (Courtesy of The Grove Archives, Glenview Park District, Glenview, Il.)

P. 33: Joseph. T. Rothrock. (Courtesy of The Grove Archives, Glenview Park District, Glenview, Il.)

P. 34: Henry W. Elliott. (Courtesy of the Smithsonian Institution Archives, RU 95, Photograph Collection, Box 7, Folder 53; Neg. # 83-6919)

P. 36: Robert Kennicott, in French trapper's costume. (Courtesy of The Grove Archives, Glenview Park District, Glenview, Il.)

P. 43: Robert Kennicott in WU uniform. (Courtesy of The Grove Archives, Glenview Park District, Glenview, Il.)

P. 46: William H. Dall in WU uniform. (Courtesy of the Smithsonian Institution Archives, RU 95, Photograph Collection, Box 6, Folder 42; Neg. #2004-18871)

P. 48: Corner Montgomery and California Streets, San Francisco, 1865. (San Francisco History Center, San Francisco Public Library)

P. 50: Cosmopolitan Hotel view, 1865. (San Francisco History Center, San Francisco Public Library)

P. 53: George Adams in WU uniform. (University of Washington Libraries, Special Collections, #UW2601)

P. 56: July 4, 1865. San Francisco parade. (San Francisco History Center, San Francisco Public Library)

P. 58: Sketch, Paddle-wheel steamer, 1865. (Courtesy of Northwestern University Archives, Kennicott-Bannister Papers, Series 11/2/2; Box 1, Folder 6, Bannister Journal Vol. 2)

P. 59: Sketch, *Golden Gate*, 1865. (Courtesy of Northwestern University Archives, Kennicott-Bannister Papers, Series 11/2/2; Box 1, Folder 6, Bannister Journal Vol. 2)

P. 65: Elliott after Dall, St. Michael's Redoubt. *Alaska and Its Resources*, 1868. (Courtesy of Smithsonian Institution Libraries, Washington, DC.)

P. 66: Russian American Company flag. New Chart of National Emblems, published by Johnson & Ward, 1868. (Courtesy of Craig Keith Design.)

P. 67: Whymper, St. Michael's 1865. (Courtesy of The Bancroft Library, Charles M. Scammon Collection, University of California, Berkley. 1950.003-B, folder 3:2)

P. 69: Whymper, Fort St. Michael's or Michaelovski. *Travel and Adventure in the Territory of Alaska,* 1868. (Courtesy of Smithsonian Institution Libraries, Washington, DC.)

P. 71: Sketch of fort plan. (Courtesy of Northwestern University Archives, Kennicott-Bannister Papers, Series 11/2/2; Box 1, Folder 6, Bannister Journal Vol. 2)

P. 73: Diary page with code. (Courtesy of Northwestern University Archives, Kennicott-Bannister Papers, Series 11/2/2; Box 1, Folder 7, Bannister Journal Vol. 3)

P. 77: Sketch of fort with three tents. (Courtesy of Smithsonian Institution Archives, RU 7073, Wm. H. Dall Papers, Box 20, diaries)

P. 79: Sketch of fort plan and room plan. (Courtesy of Smithsonian Institution Archives, RU 7073, Wm. H. Dall Papers, Box 2, Scrapbook.)

P. 80: Male Parka. *Travel and Adventure in the Territory of Alaska,* 1868. (Courtesy of Smithsonian Institution Libraries, Washington, DC.)

P. 82: Whymper, Arrival at Frozen Yukon. *Travel and Adventure in the Territory of Alaska,* 1868. (Courtesy of Smithsonian Institution Libraries, Washington, DC.)

P. 85: Whymper, Aural Light, Nulato. *Travel and Adventure in the Territory of Alaska,* 1868. (Courtesy of Smithsonian Institution Libraries, Washington, DC.)

P. 87: Snowshoe. *Travel and Adventure in the Territory of Alaska,* 1868. (Courtesy of Smithsonian Institution Libraries, Washington, DC.)

P. 88: Compass and cover. Photo by Steve Swanson. ©The Grove (Courtesy of The Grove Archives, Glenview Park District, Glenview, Il.)

P. 89: Map sketch with instructions. (Courtesy of Smithsonian Institution Archives, RU 7073, Wm. H. Dall Papers, Box 31, Folder 1; Neg. # 79-14810)

P. 92: Map sketch, unexplored. (Courtesy of Smithsonian Institution Archives, RU 7073, Wm. H. Dall Papers, Box 2, Scrapbook.)

P. 93: Sketch of fort. (Courtesy of Smithsonian Institution Archives, RU 7073, Wm. H. Dall Papers, Box 2, Scrapbook.)

P. 99: Diary margin sketch. (University of Washington Libraries, Special Collections, #UW235382.)

P. 100: Elliott after Dall, Interior of Ft. Derabin. *Alaska and Its Resources*, 1868. (Courtesy of Smithsonian Institution Libraries, Washington, DC.)

P. 101: Whymper, Yukon Spring Ice Break Up. *Travel and Adventure in the Territory of Alaska,* 1868. (Courtesy of Smithsonian Institution Libraries, Washington, DC.)

P. 102: Block house, St. Michael's. (Richard Frank Photograph Collection; Archives, Alaska and Polar Regions Collections, Rasmuson Library, Univ. of Alaska Fairbanks)

P. 110: Steamship souvenir card. (Courtesy of Northwestern University Archives, Kennicott-Bannister Papers, Series 11/2/2; Box 1, Folder 7)

P. 111: Wm. Stimpson. (National Portrait Gallery, Smithsonian Institution/ Art Resource, NY. NPG 78.110)

P. 112: Kennicott family grave site. Photo by Steve Swanson. ©The Grove (Courtesy of The Grove Archives, Glenview Park District, Glenview, Il.)

P. 113: Robert Kennicott's tombstone. Photo by Steve Swanson. ©The Grove (Courtesy of The Grove Archives, Glenview Park District, Glenview, Il.)

P. 118: Robert Kennicott engraving. (Courtesy of the Smithsonian Institution Archives, RU 95, Photograph Collection, Box 14, Folder 39; Neg # 2004-18874.)

P. 124: Diary page with code. (Courtesy of Northwestern University Archives, Kennicott-Bannister Papers, Series 11/2/2; Box 1, Folder 7, Bannister Journal Vol .3)

P. 133: Sleeve Ribbons. Photo by Steve Swanson ©The Grove (Courtesy of The Grove Archives, Glenview Park District, Glenview, Il.)

P. 136: Kennicott's owl. *Alaska and Its Resources*, 1868. (Courtesy of Smithsonian Institution Libraries, Washington, DC.)

P. 145: Scientific Corps Flag. *Alaska and Its Resources*, 1868. (Courtesy of Smithsonian Institution Libraries, Washington, DC.)

Maps

P. 18-19: Insert from Map of Yukon or Kvichpak River. *Travel and Adventure in the Territory of Alaska,* 1868. (Courtesy of Smithsonian Institution Libraries, Washington, DC.) Routes added by Craig Keith Design, 2010.

P. 74-75: Russian Possessions map, Yukon River; Rare Maps Collection, G3351 P92, section 3; Archives, Alaska and Polar Regions Collections, Rasmuson Library, University of Alaska Fairbanks

P. 74 Yukon River Map. *Travel and Adventure in the Territory of Alaska,* 1868. (Courtesy of Smithsonian Institution Libraries, Washington, DC.)

P. 75 North Western America from Port Clarence to Mouth of Kvichpak River. Library of Congress, Geography and Maps Division, G4372.N5P5, 1864-67.

Index